AF522008

Kim Dickey *Words Are Leaves*

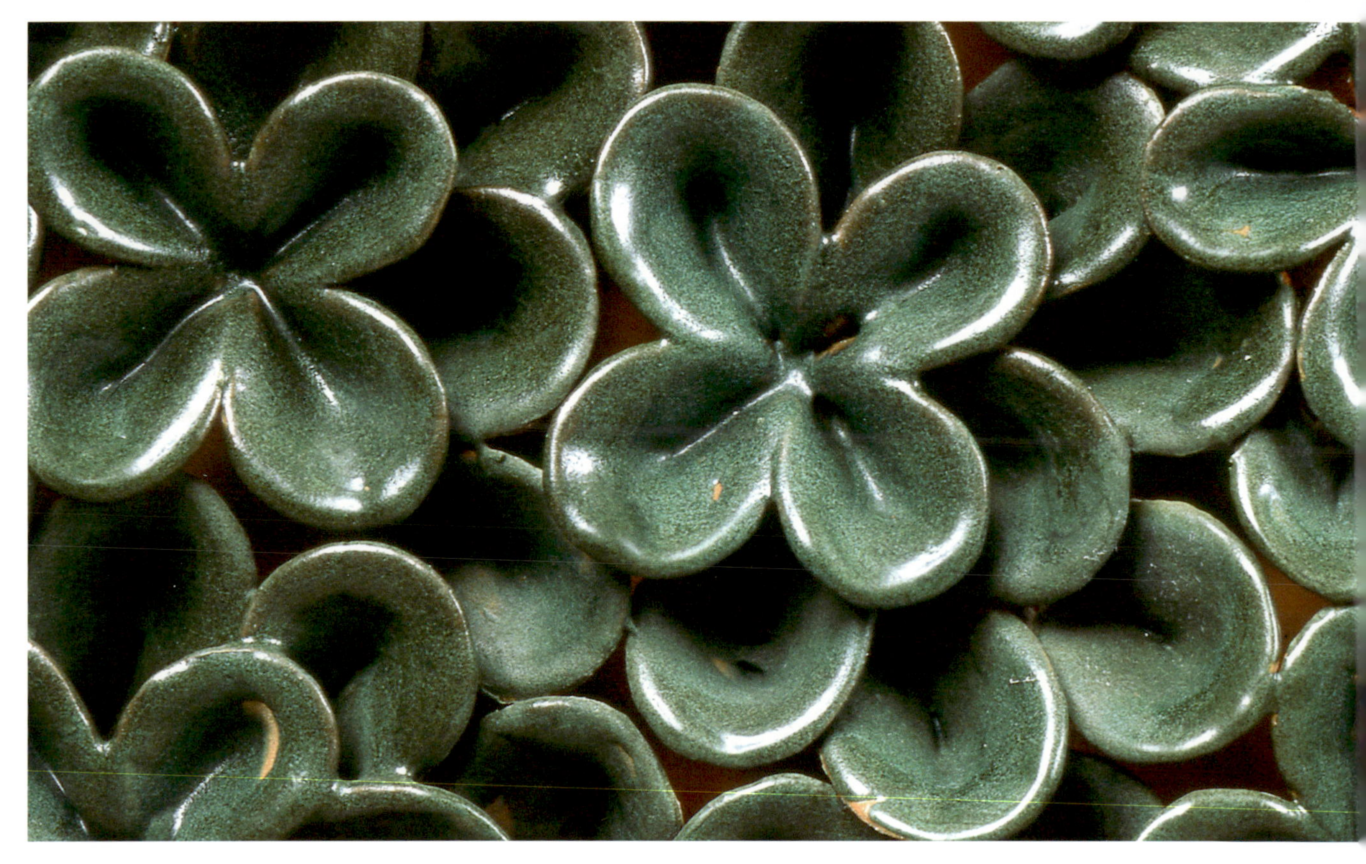

Kim Dickey

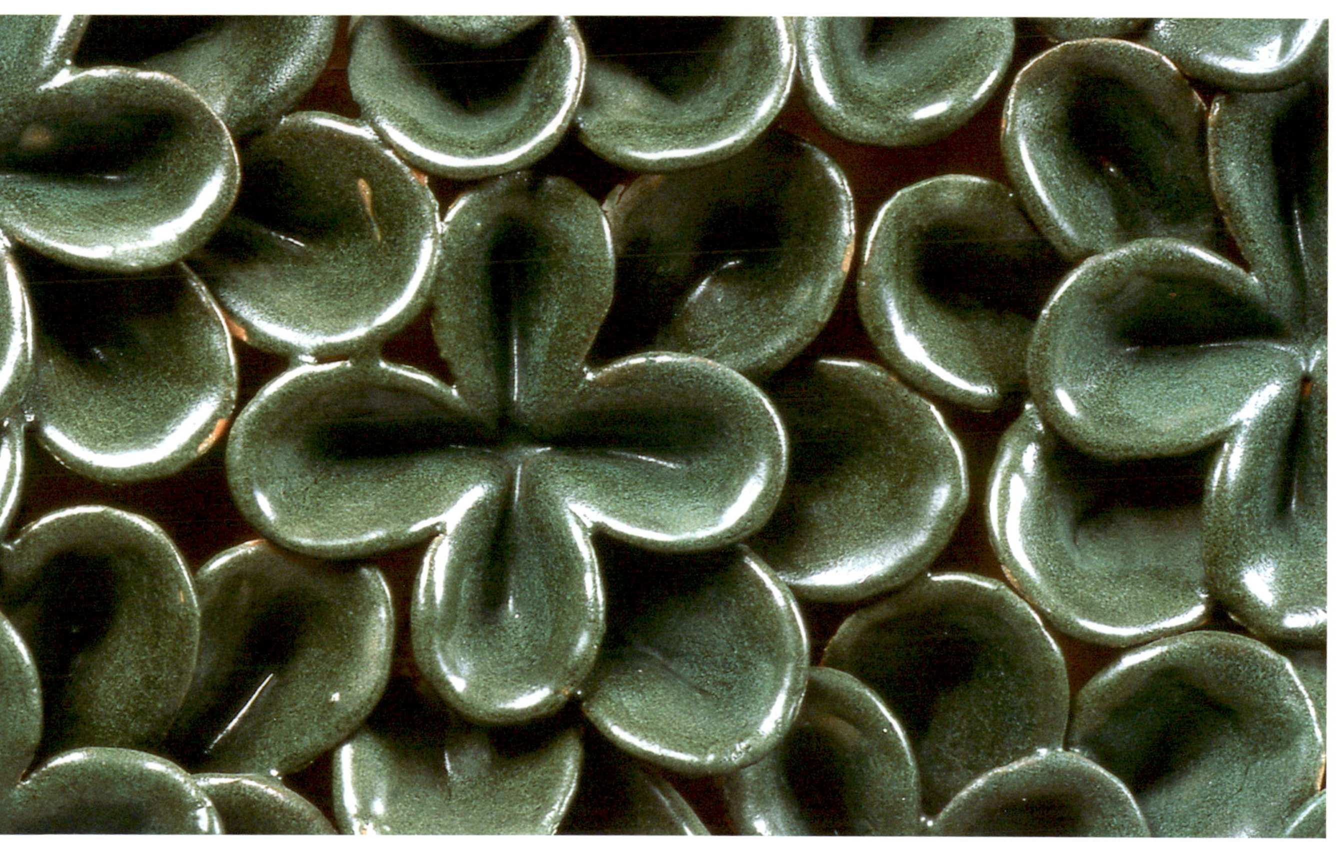

EDITED BY
Nora Burnett Abrams

WITH CONTRIBUTIONS BY
Glenn Adamson
Elissa Auther
Lisa Tamiris Becker
Ezra Shales
and an interview with the artist

MUSEUM OF CONTEMPORARY ART DENVER

Words Are Leaves

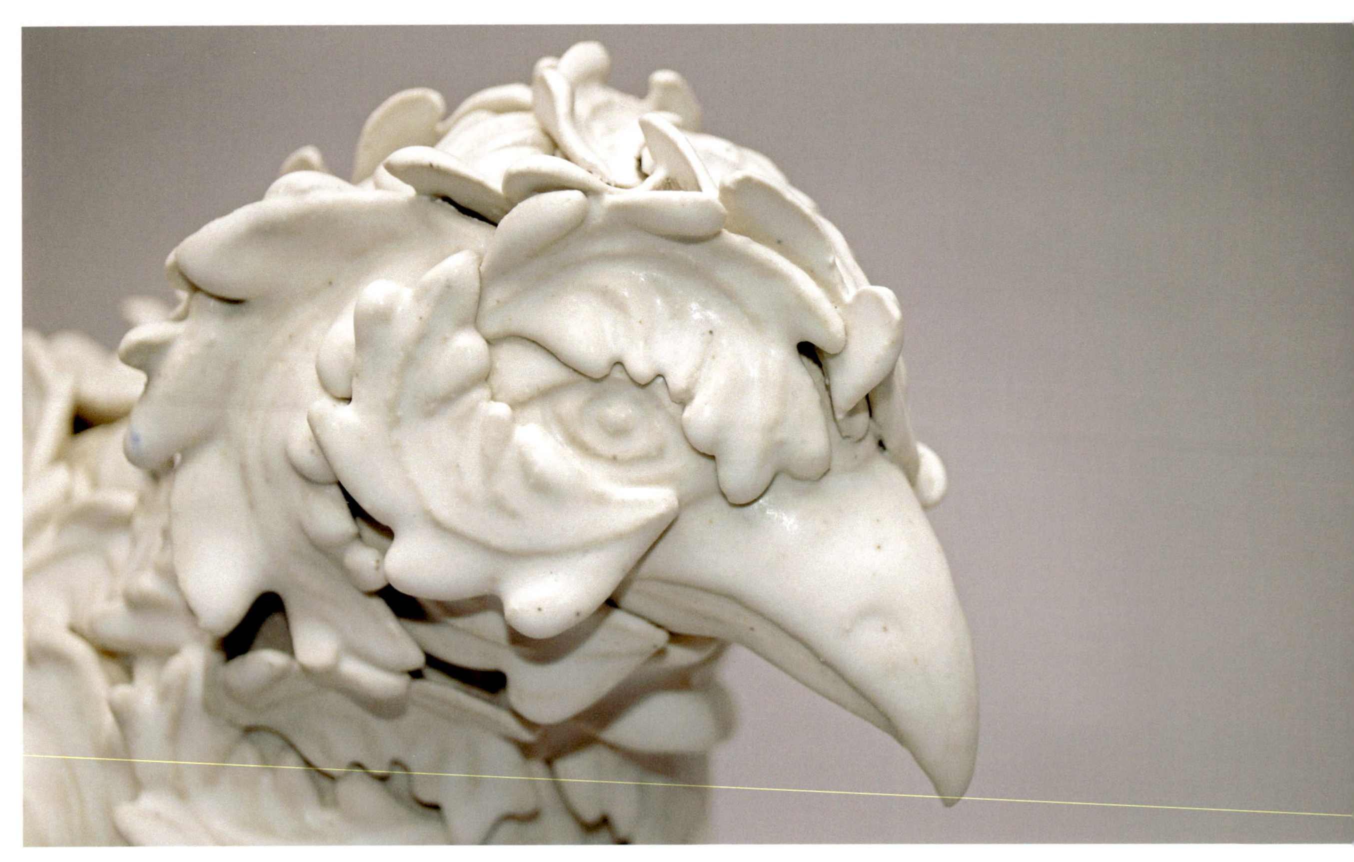

Contents

Foreword

What do William Morris and Robert Morris have in common? That's right: Kim Dickey. In one imposing series of sculptures, she appropriated geometric forms suggesting empty plinths and platforms from the minimalist sculptor Robert Morris and then festooned them—*lovingly*, I want to say—with delicate vegetation reminiscent of Arts and Crafts designer William Morris's wallpapers. As so often in Dickey's oeuvre, these works see her taking up the false binaries of art history (fine and decorative, rigorous and beautiful, geometric and organic, ornamental and monumental, abstract and representational) and slamming them irreverently together. Implicitly, but insistently, she poses the question of how we ever came to view these things as opposed in the first place.

Many artists have a characteristic maneuver: a pattern of thinking that threads throughout their work. William Morris's was to reach back into the past and offer his findings as models for an alternative, more glorious modernity. Robert Morris's was to expose the underlying codes of the artistic process. Dickey's is to take a step back and see the bigger picture. Diverse as her works may be, they all share a concern with the beneficial effects of distance. Hers is a circumspect and evaluative gaze, which takes in not only the art object but also its surrounding context.

Dickey's interest in the dynamics of detachment is sometimes expressed literally, as in her bird's-eye portrayals of garden parterres, or through her use of film (which gives access to an object while withholding its actual presence). Almost always, it is also expressed historically, in that she typically builds from preexisting stylistic and formal components. In this exhibition, you will find references not only to the two Morrises, but also to myriad other precursors in architecture, tapestry, garden design, and handcraft, including the self-styled "mad potter of Biloxi" George Ohr, from whom she borrows the project's title. Historical points of reference function for Dickey much as props do for a playwright, to propel her narratives: "to set a stage," as she puts it, "upon which memories, nostalgia, and imagination can play."

Distance also operates in deeper, more metaphorical registers in Dickey's work. It is evident, for example, in her attitude toward the ceramic medium. While she is masterful in this most primary of materials, she aligns herself with the theorist Jacques Rancière, who argues that disciplinarity is inherently exclusionary. Only a fluid practice can achieve what he calls "a poetic knowledge" that transcends specialist concerns. Many artists try to seduce through the beauty, skill, scale, and content that are particular to their chosen medium. All of these variables are present in Dickey's work, too, but they never ingratiate. They are more like citations than demonstrations, transient allusions within an expanded, and expansive, field.

Earlier in her career, Dickey staged a performance during an exhibition called *Holding Patterns: Objects in Action*, in which members of the public were invited to draw objects from a stranger's garment. In this interaction, an intimate space—someone's pocket—became uncomfortably yet tantalizingly available. Dickey re-creates that performance as part of her show in Denver. It is a reminder that distance of various kinds (psychological, physical, temporal) is always already there, all around us. Her characteristic maneuver is to use that distance much as she uses clay. Yet somehow the result becomes quite the opposite: an opportunity to see something clearly, to truly connect.

Glenn Adamson

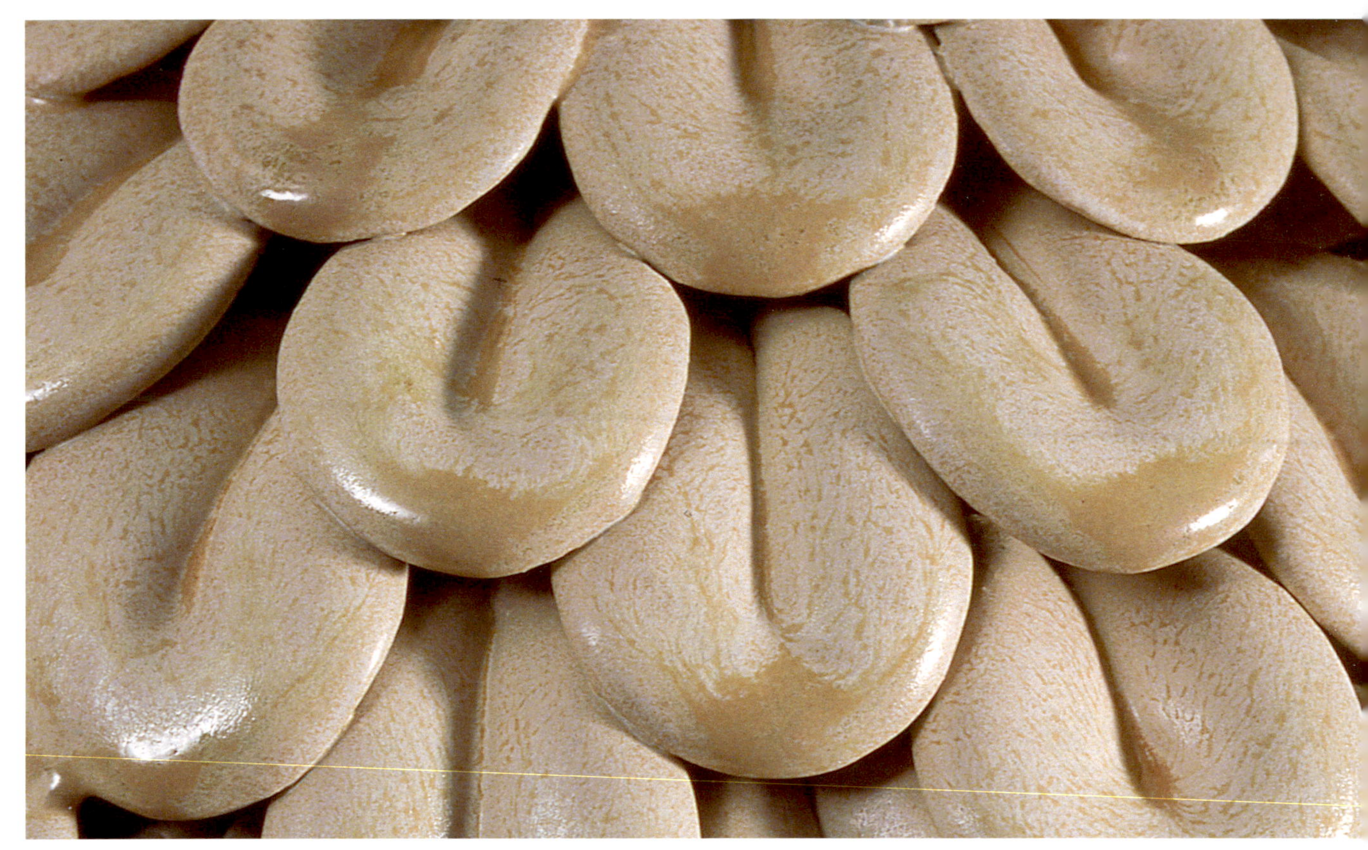

Sense and Sensorium

The Art of Kim Dickey

Lisa Tamiris Becker

Thus the antiquarian seeks to both distance and appropriate the past. In order to entertain an antiquarian sensibility, a rupture in historical consciousness must have occurred, creating a sense that one can make one's own culture other —distant and discontinuous.

From "Objects of Desire" in Susan Stewarts, *On Longing: Narratives of the Miniature, the Gigantic, the Souvenir, the Collection.*[1]

Kim Dickey's evocative work simultaneously engages both our sensorium and our intellect. The tension produced by her minimalist, platonic forms—for instance, rectangular sculptural hedges, or omphalos-like mounded shrubs and bushes—and her covering of those forms with dense, decorative leaves and flowers leads us to experience a heightened sense of visual and visceral delight. The works elicit desire, memory, and a longing for touch, taste, aroma, and sensual pleasure. At the same time, her thoughtful allusions to art history, ceramic history, and the history of gardens, for instance the formal gardens of the French Enlightenment, medieval foliate forms, as well as midcentury modernism and minimalist sculpture, heighten our intellectual curiosity and engagement.

Her ceramic sculptures function like theatrical props (at times literally so) and prompt an awareness of both larger history and personal longing. In *Forever panting* (2006), for instance, a potted bush composed of tongues tantalizes, its sumptuous satin glaze enticing our erotic desire for touch and the sensuality of the oral. Her *Salad Plate* series of prints (2003), a set of four plate-like compositions of geometrically interwoven tongues, fingers, lips, and noses, respectively, conjures the senses associated with each of these body parts as they engage in the act of eating.

Other examples of her work such as her carpets depicting imagined formal gardens, or her carefully composed photographs of *allées* and hedges at Versailles and Villandry, likewise offer up a stage for a bedazzled sensorium combined with mindful curiosity. Dickey employs poetic tropes at various scales, from twenty-foot-long wall works to hedges covered in leaves and flowers to miniature shrubs composed of tongue-like leaves or bouquets.

One might read Dickey's work as an effort to feminize the minimalist tradition. Her hedge- and shrub-like forms

Forever panting (detail), 2006.
Glazed porcelain and concrete,
45 × 14 inches.

Photograph by Jeff Wells.

challenge the cool steel and glass geometries of Robert Morris, Donald Judd, or Tony Smith by covering their iconic forms in patterns of ceramic flowers. The decorative becomes paramount, as all becomes engulfed in leaf or bloom. One example is *Inverted L Beam #2* (2011), in which she transforms one of Morris's massive L-beams into a hedge-like sculpture.

Dickey's early work includes handmade female urinals or *Lady Js* (1994–99), which allow a woman to urinate while standing. These ceramic vessels are elegantly designed to direct the flow of the urine into single or multiple streams, inspiring a kind of formal delight in the most everyday of bodily functions, while also offering their users new options for urinating while standing. Dickey often accompanies these objects with photographs revealing the objects in use.

In her early video work *The Fall* (2000), a character Dickey describes as the Devil is served a multicourse meal on a stacked-up, handmade place setting. The primeval but elegantly coursed meal, in which the crustacean-like serving dishes are almost indistinguishable from their edible contents, becomes a metaphor for dark desires. The Devil character, played by Peter Halasz, devours one course after another, imbibing and consuming the delicacies with increasing intensity. The noirish quality of *The Fall* captures an ironic tension in which pleasure and desire are intertwined with lasciviousness and bloodthirsty consumption.

In her performance works, Dickey engages with the sensuality of the body as animated by clothing and elements hidden within it. *Pocket Lady: You Only Have One Chance* (2000) was performed at the opening of her exhibition *Holding Patterns: Objects in Action* at Rule Gallery in Denver in 2000 and involved an anonymous performer wearing a red velvet dress composed of forty pockets; members of the audience were invited to reach into the pockets to retrieve hidden objects. "This intrusion into the space of a stranger," the artist says, "something rarely allowed, briefly breached the common barrier between desire and distance. The dress with its hidden recesses and objects—each of which related to the theme of holding patterns—was a tactile sculpture on this single evening."[2] In a more recent work, *Rest Assured, X Boyfriends* (2014), Dickey made a quilt out of the back pockets of men's jeans, each pocket containing a single, wrapped condom. The implicit and explicit eroticism of the hidden condoms elicits erotic desire on the part of the viewer, conjuring both the dangers and the pleasures associated with sexuality. In both of

Inverted L Beam #2, 2011.
Aluminum, glazed terracotta, silicone, and rubber grommets, 78 × 137½ × 17 inches.

Photograph courtesy the artist.

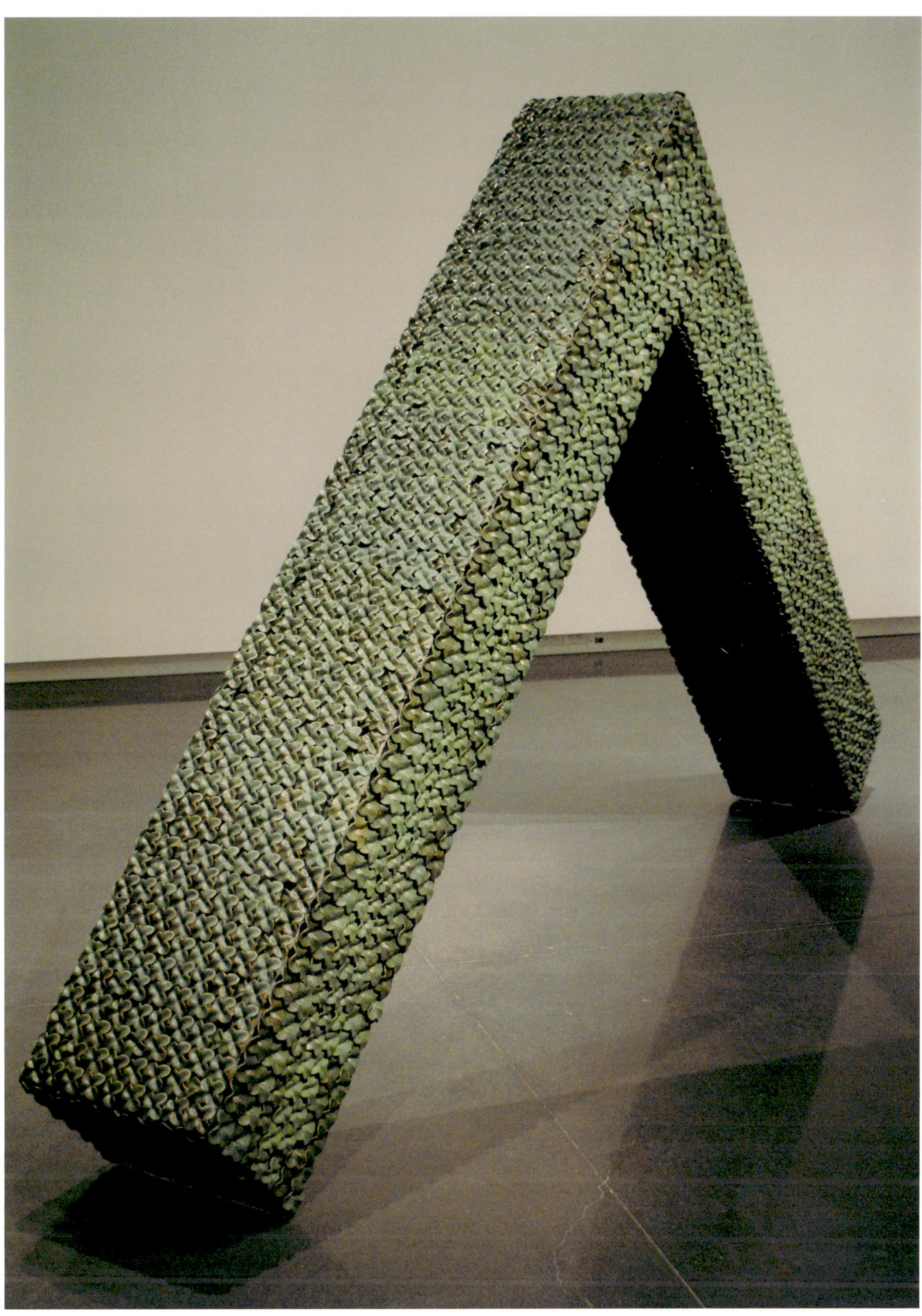

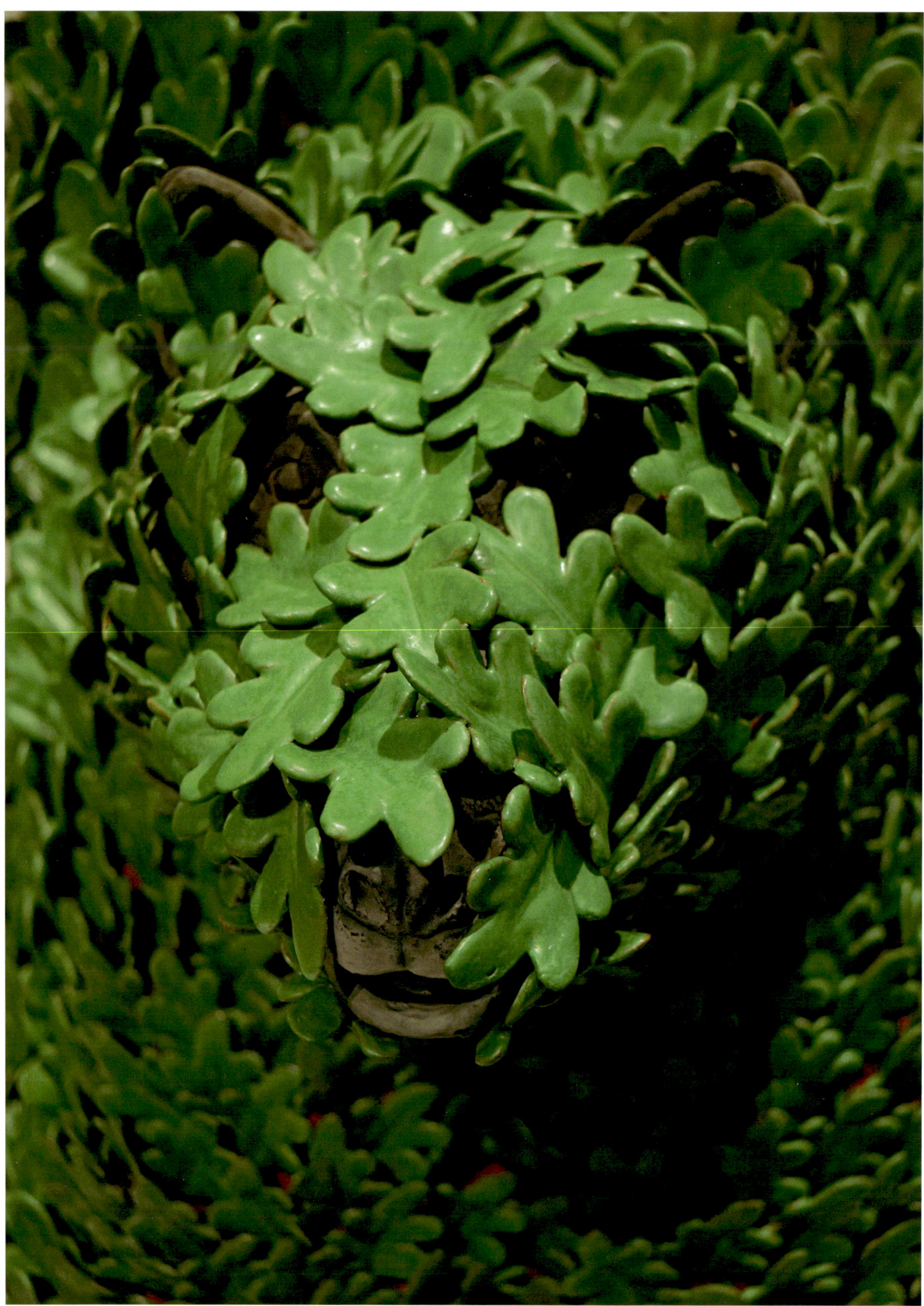

these works, the viewer is enthralled by a yearning to both behold the work and to touch something carefully hidden within it. The clothing becomes an interstitial space between the body and its surrounding field and audience.

Foliated Forms and Beings

However paradoxical this may seem, it is often this inner immensity that gives their real meaning to certain expressions concerning the visible world. To take a precise example, we might make a detailed examination of what is meant by the immensity of the forest. For this "immensity" originates in a body of impressions which, in reality, have little connection with geographical information. We do not have to be long in the woods to experience the always rather anxious impression of "going deeper and deeper" into a limitless world.

—Gaston Bachelard, *The Poetics of Space*[3]

In a few recent works, Dickey renders in simple, elegant white ceramic, animals covered in leaves. The titles include *Wolfgang's Lion* (2011), *The Departure* (2011), *Travelling Companion (Endurance)* (2015), *Unguarded (Vulnerability)* (2015), *Clan Champion (Probity after Robert Frost)* (2015), and *Quick Cony (Timeliness)* (2015). The foliated lions, camels, stags, and rabbits are discrete sculptural objects, which she sometimes arranges into complex installations that include her green shrubs and walls. The creatures reference icons of ceramic history, such as Chinese Tang dynasty camels, while also invoking mystical human-animal relationships and the decorative creature motifs found in medieval cloisters. Unlike the painterly glazing of the Tang dynasty camels, however, these works are devoid of color.

By contrast, in several works from 2015 she evokes the enigmatic medieval "green man" or foliate head that appears in medieval churches across Europe, known as *der grüne Mann* in Germany or *tête de feuilles*, *cracheur de feuilles*, or *masque feuillu* in France. Dickey's version of the mysterious "green man" emerges from sculptures of green ceramic leaves situated alongside arrangements of minimalist beams transformed into hedges. These biomorphic shrubs challenge the imagination and remind us that the foliage covering the forms is deeply rooted in a historical tradition of the medieval decorative imaginary, not minimalist austerity.

For her exhibition at the Museum of Contemporary Art Denver, Dickey has created a new installation involving her foliated animals, placed in the gallery in an elliptical

Blending into Attention (detail), 2015.
Glazed terracotta, 37 × 31 × 27 inches.

Photograph courtesy the artist.

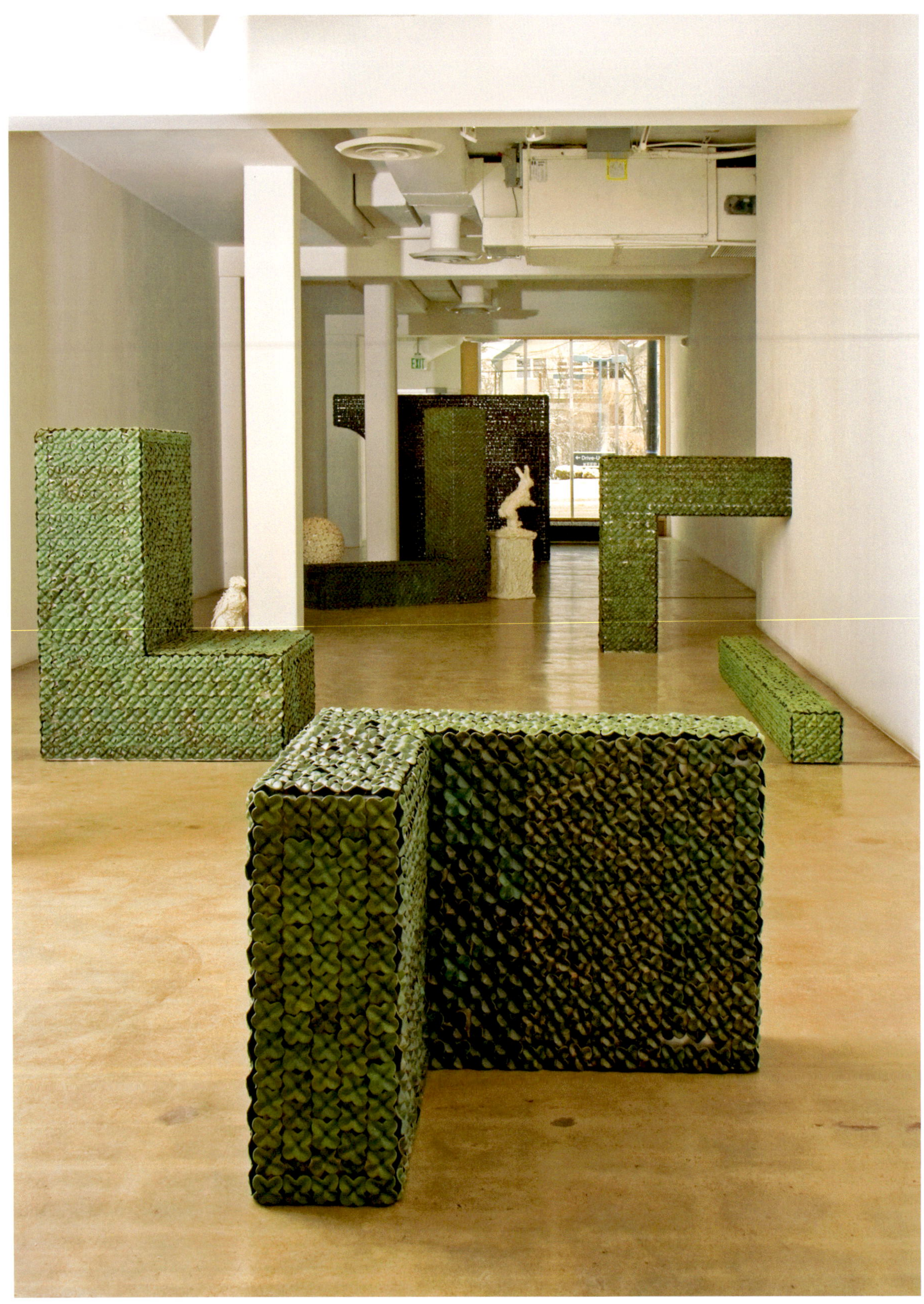

FACING PAGE

All is Leaf, installation view, Rule Gallery, Denver, 2011. Seven aluminum wall forms and four stoneware foliate figures.

Photograph by Jeff Wells.

RIGHT

The Departure, 2011.
Glazed stoneware, 45 × 20 × 14 inches.

Photograph by Jeff Wells.

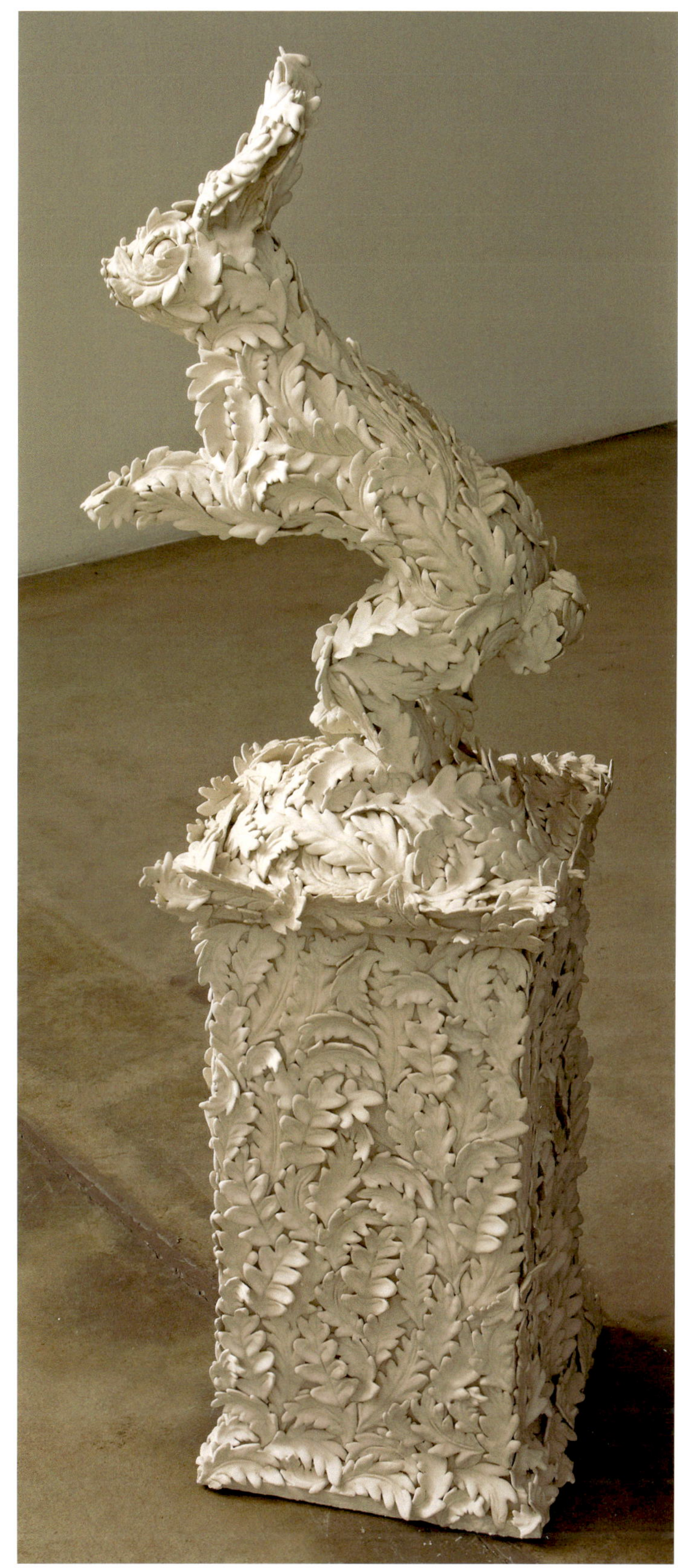

configuration. She has also wrapped the walls with a graphite drawing of a continuous knotted line, the patterns of which are derived from those carved into the walls of Portuguese Romanesque churches. Dickey states, "These works in tandem are meant to create a space of consciousness and interiority, like a cloister, where what is reflected in the architecture and sculpture is the evidence of an internal struggle made external."[4]

In an adjacent space, a series of glazed, shield-like forms draws on imagery from a fifteenth-century French tapestry of a rabbit hunt found in the Burrell Collection in Glasgow. The imagery includes rabbit warren holes, netting, escaping rabbits, and captured rabbits presented as fragments in a salon-style hanging. The artist states that the work is intended to "allude to the elusive nature of consciousness and memory," while also serving as a reminder of one's own fallibility. These masculine, shield-like forms contrast with lush wall works such as *Succulent* (2000), which according to Dickey "mask and reclaim the emblematic (male) forms."[5]

Dickey's works are typically monochromatic, in white or green. But occasionally a broader spectrum of color enters, as in her recent *Fading Bouquet* (2015), in which blooms emerge from white pinched stoneware vases. The blooms are bulbous, egglike, and glazed with floral patterns that recall popular textiles of the 1950s and 1960s. The pinched vases are similar to Dickey's works from 2000 such as *Havisham Bride*, but color now emerges from the forms, creating poetics and erotics of dissipating beauty; they remind us of the transience and fragility of color, and, ultimately, of life. Like *memento mori*, these works bring together strength and fragility, purity and impurity, reminding us of the delicate balance of life in which every bright bouquet is destined to eventually fade away.

Fading Bouquet, 2015.
Glazed stoneware, 32 × 15 inches.

Photograph courtesy the artist.

NOTES

1. Susan Stewart, *On Longing: Narratives of the Miniature, the Gigantic, the Souvenir, the Collection* (Durham, NC: Duke University Press, 1999), 142.

2. Kim Dickey, exhibition statement, http://www.kimdickeystudio.com/Project_pgs/11_holdingpatterns_menu.html.

3. Gaston Bachelard, *The Poetics of Space*, trans. Maria Jolas (Boston: Beacon Press, 1969), 185.

4. Kim Dickey, email to the author, April 22, 2016.

5. Ibid.

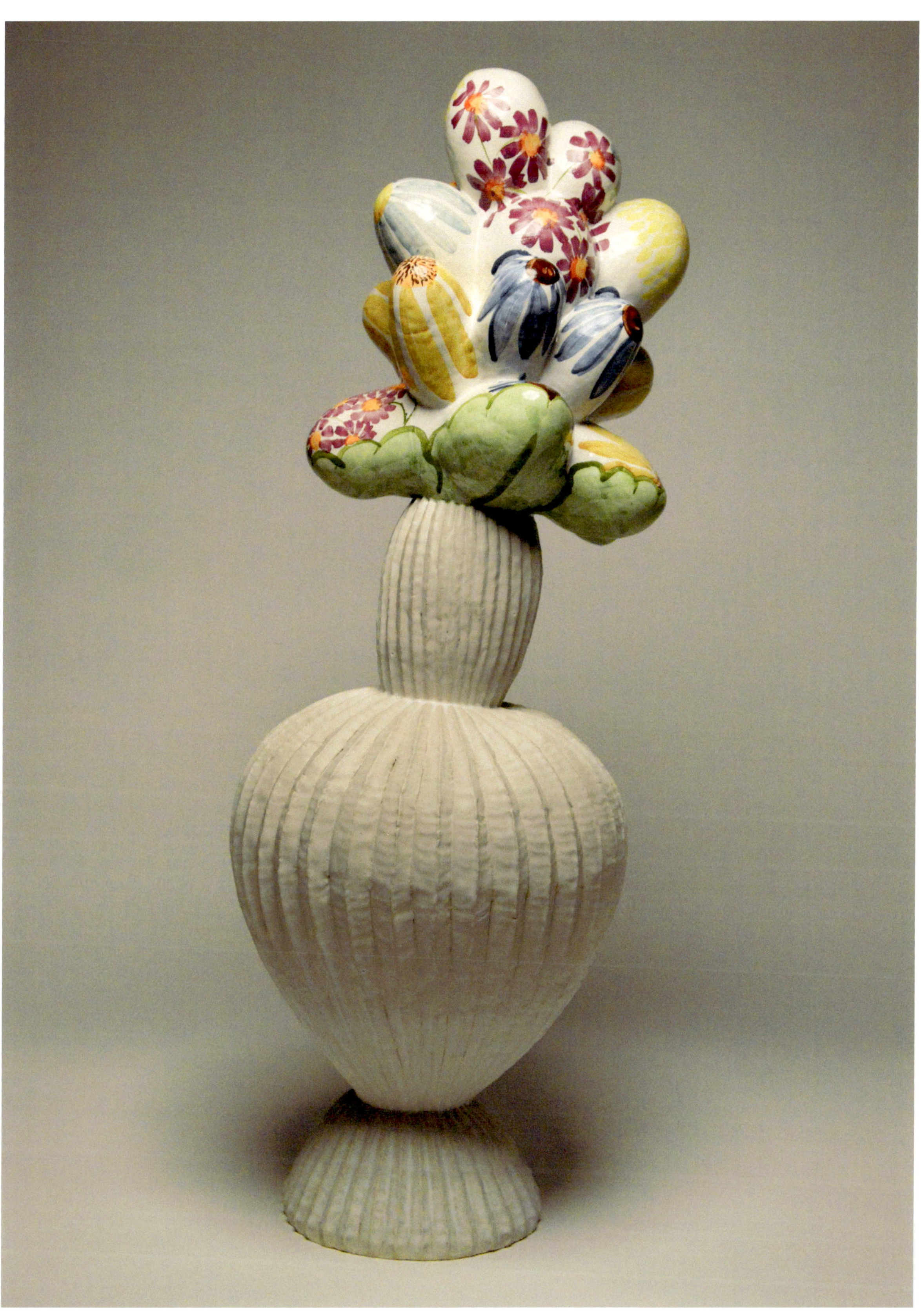

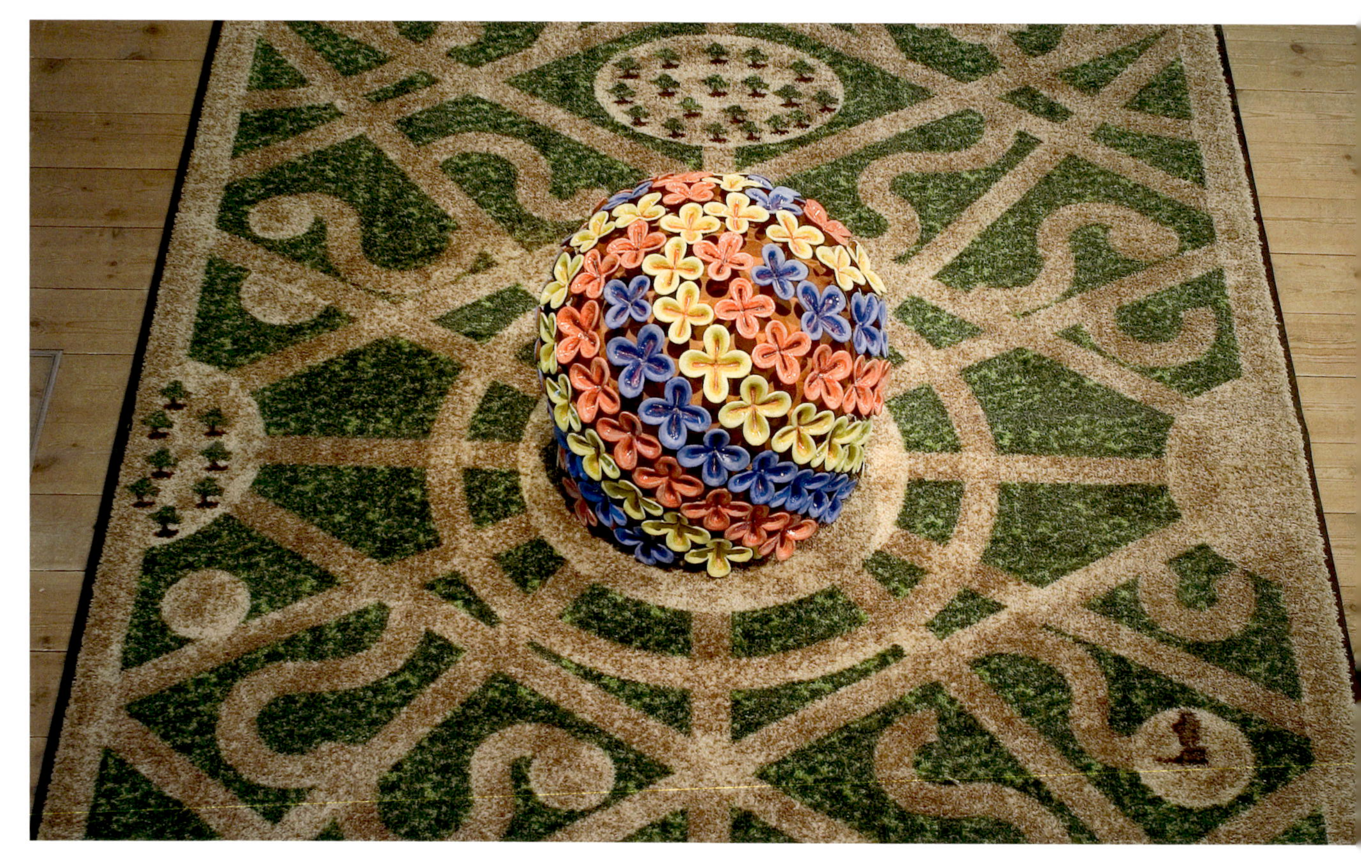

Kim Dickey's Minimalist *Bocage*

Elissa Auther

On a research trip to France in 2001, Kim Dickey began to conceptualize a body of work inspired by the *jardin à la française*, the magnificent formal gardens of the seventeenth and eighteenth centuries known for their symmetrical organization and carefully clipped vegetation.[1] The sculptures and installations that were directly inspired by the trip, including *Bushes* (2002–8), *Knots* (2005), *Cold Pastoral* (2007), *All is Leaf* (2011), and *Mille-fleur* (2011), engage in a creative dialogue with these formal gardens, responding to their weirdly attractive artificiality, the theatrical elements of surprise in their design, and the fantasies—from the wistful to the erotic—they enabled in their bygone *habitués*. Highlighted in this series of works is the human urge for mastery over nature, for the transformation of nature into culture, rendered all the more abstract through the medium of clay, which freezes their forms permanently.

In drawing upon the striking geometries of the formal French garden and its unnatural cultivation of shrubs, hedges, and trees into elemental, perfected forms, Dickey calls attention to the very sculptural quality of these gardens—what the contemporary viewer might refer to as their minimalist aesthetic. Dickey's work takes advantage of this intriguing relationship to minimalist sculpture and extends it to broader considerations, including its antagonistic relationship to the decorative. Through witty references to both minimalist art and the decorative arts, her work cleverly activates cultural and aesthetic oppositions that challenge our very understanding of what counts as fine art.

Bushes consists of a group of bulbous shrubs mounted on low pedestals. Here Dickey investigates not only the aesthetic fashioning of plants into ideal shapes, but also the eighteenth-century craze for rococo *bocage*, the amassment of porcelain flowers and branches for artificial bouquets and the embellishment of chandeliers, clocks, potpourri containers, mirrors, vessels, and figures. The term—literally meaning "grove" or "thicket"—was earlier applied to the arbor-like stage scenery of the 1750s, from whence came the use of branches and flowers as backdrops for porcelain figures, and then the foliage as applied to all manner of interior furnishings. The art historian Mimi Hellman, in an essay that likens the popularity of porcelain *bocage* as applied to furnishings to the garnish placed beside a fine meal, describes this ceramic tradition as a complex tension between nature and artifice: "Ultimately, porcelain flowers produced what Roland Barthes would call a reality effect: an insistent accumulation of acutely rendered details

Beauty Bush on *Radiate* from *Knots*, 2005. Glazed terracotta sculpture, 19 × 19 inches; printed industrial rug, 6 × 10 feet.

Photograph courtesy Skulpturens Hus, Stockholm.

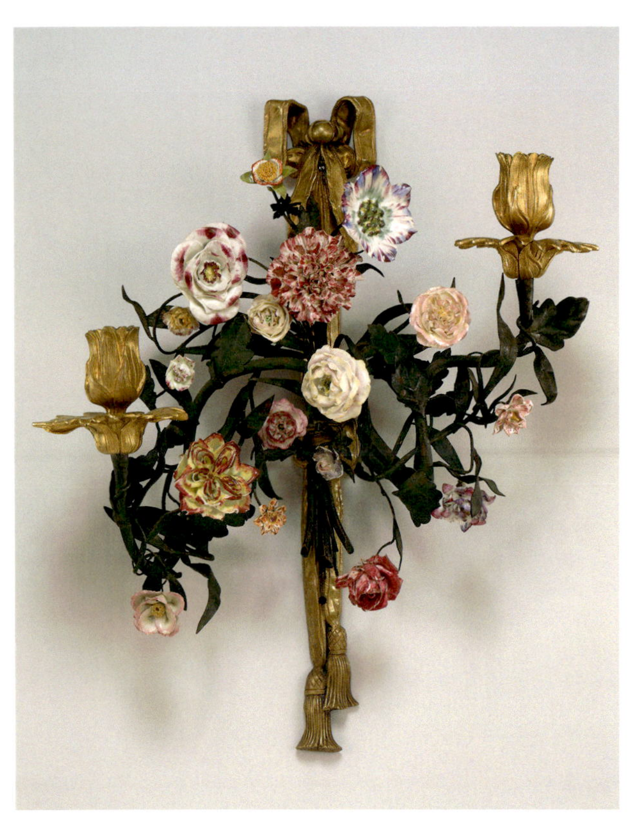

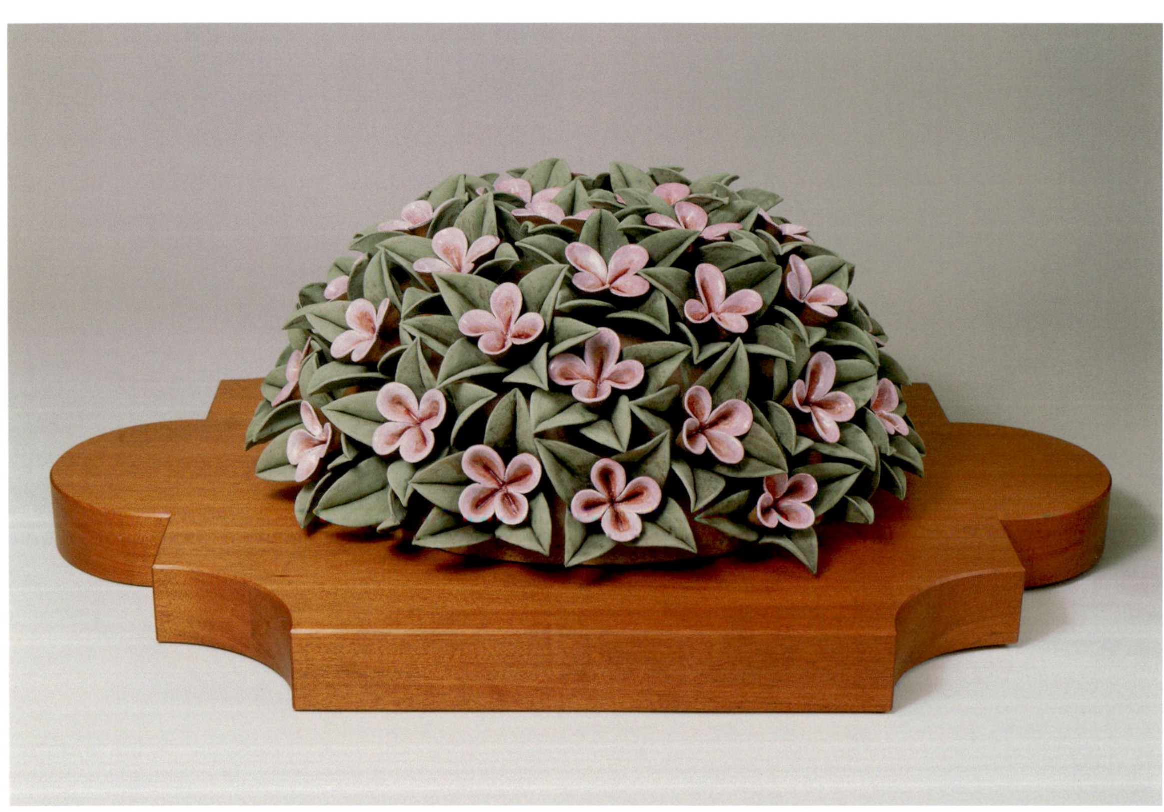

that claim transparent correspondence with their referents, but in fact signify the *idea* of the real rather than denoting it directly."[2]

In the case of the works that comprise *Bushes*, Dickey reinterprets *bocage* by highlighting its appeal to the ideal in balance with the real. Rather than adhering to the tradition of porcelain *bocage*'s miniaturization of the flower or branch, in *Bushes* there is a scale shift: here we have the decorative at real-life size. The surfaces of the *Bushes* are covered with hundreds of ceramic leaves, buds, and flowers, yet they are not detailed, illusionistic replicas of foliage, but rather consist of a limited vocabulary of stylized quatrefoils, spear-like leaves, and star-shaped petals. In concert with their elementary spherical shapes, the allover, repetitively patterned surfaces of the *Bushes* promote an ideal of perfection imagined in the mind of the gardener. On close inspection, this idealized expression is counterbalanced by the imperfect character of each individual, hand-crafted yet repetitive element. The balanced tension that *Bushes* maintains between perfection and imperfection is one of the most important themes of Dickey's practice, related to the relationship between sculpture and decoration. Conventionally understood as the antithesis of sculpture, decoration and its association with practices such as *bocage* are central to the marginal status of ceramics in the history of art. In *Bushes*, Dickey deliberately collapses decoration and sculpture in order to question their historical opposition.

Today, landscape design is conventionally viewed as an applied form of outdoor ornamentation, secondary to the more important art of architecture. By contrast, in the seventeenth and eighteenth centuries, "the science of landscape" was defined as a fine art form, along with poetry and painting, its "sister arts."[3] Likewise ceramics enjoyed respect as a high art form, fueled by the craze for porcelain in Europe from the Renaissance through the eighteenth century. Yet, like garden design, it too descended the aesthetic ladder, first to the position of "decorative" sculpture and then, under modernism, to kitsch, as craft crystallized as a category subordinate to fine art. But Dickey is not attempting to restore ceramic sculpture to its once-honored place as a fine art form, nor to nullify garden design's second-class status. Rather, in works such as *Rosebud Bush* (2002) and *Tart Bush* (2002) from the *Bushes* series, she calls attention to the very aspects of ceramics and garden design —their status as decoration or ornamentation—responsible for their marginal place within the art world. Dickey further

Wall light (detail), ca. 1750–1760.
Gilt bronze, painted iron, soft- and hard-paste porcelain, 22½ inches (height).

The Jack and Belle Linsky Collection, 1982 (1982.60.85). The Metropolitan Museum of Art. Photograph © The Metropolitan Museum of Art, courtesy Art Resource, NY.

Rosebud Bush, 2002.
Glazed terracotta and mahogany, 27 × 51 inches.

Photograph by Nick Havholm.

anchors their forms within the discourse of the decorative through the use of low platforms in shapes that recall design motifs of the *jardin à la français*, reiterating the artificial nature of the sculpted plant. On the surface, it might look like these works merely revel in the decorative as a form of updated but culturally irrelevant *bocage*. But in Dickey's hands, the decorative is an investigative tool used to shed light on how aesthetic value is constructed through hierarchies and oppositions separating sculpture from forms and styles defined as "non-art."

Dickey is not the first artist to take on the subject of the low position of ceramics in the history of art, but her contribution with *Bushes* and subsequent related works is unique. A comparison to the work of Robert Arneson, arguably the first contemporary artist to take issue with ceramic sculpture's second-class status, is illuminating here. As Glenn Adamson has demonstrated, Arneson held conflicting attitudes toward the art/craft divide that consigned ceramics to the realm of non-art. He was known to quip, "Ceramics is the world's most interesting hobby," and to describe his working process as akin to Betty Crocker in the kitchen.[4] Yet he also tried to "treat ceramics as an art and this meant ... deal[ing] with ideas and content."[5] Arneson also expressed this contradictory tension through a style and subject matter that reveled in the amateur and the decorative. His *John with Art* (1964), in which clay is associated with excrement and porcelain bathroom fixtures, or his simple clay bricks, are the best-known examples of this approach. In addition, Arneson created a number of works in low-fire earthenware that directly reference ceramics' associations with kitsch, including flowerpots and flowers, cookie jars, and trophy-like figurines. His humble pop art sculptures are casually and at times eccentrically modeled, giving them a humorous, quirky personality accentuated by Arneson's brash use of color. Making a mockery of popular ceramic traditions and styles allowed Arneson to personally and professionally negotiate the demoralizing status of the potter and the hierarchy of art and craft that dismisses ceramics as a lesser practice.

Dickey's practice is likewise a conscious investigation of artistic hierarchies, but her interest in this issue and the way she carries it out differ from Arneson's in important ways. Arneson's *Ceramic Rose* (1968–69) embodies all the amateur associations with clay the artist loved, with its sloppy, unsophisticated modeling, gaudy glaze, and associations with commercially produced ceramic tchotchkes, whereas Dickey's

Pomegranate Tree, 2007.
Glazed terracotta on limestone,
40 × 28 inches.

Photograph courtesy Studio Penumbra.

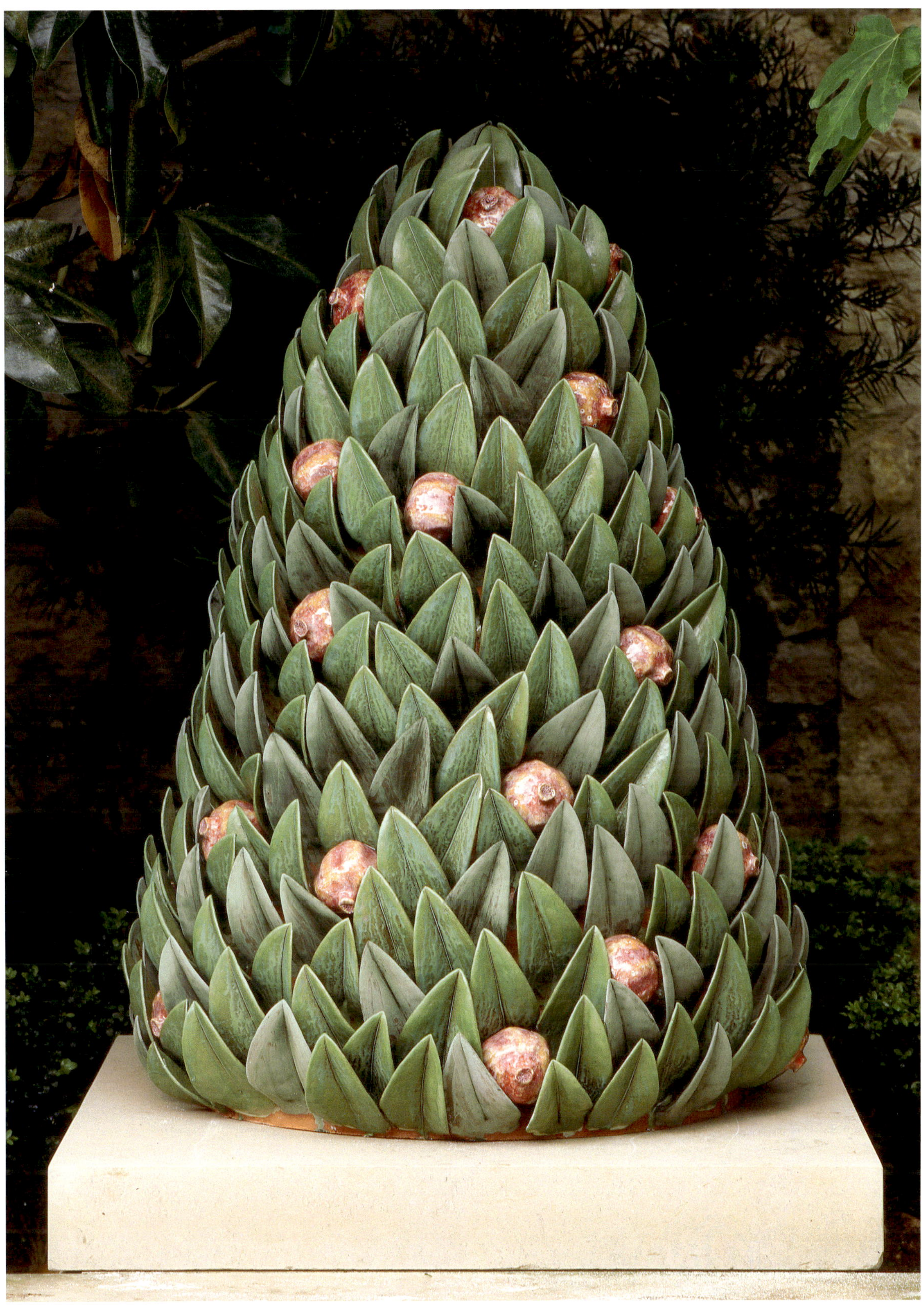

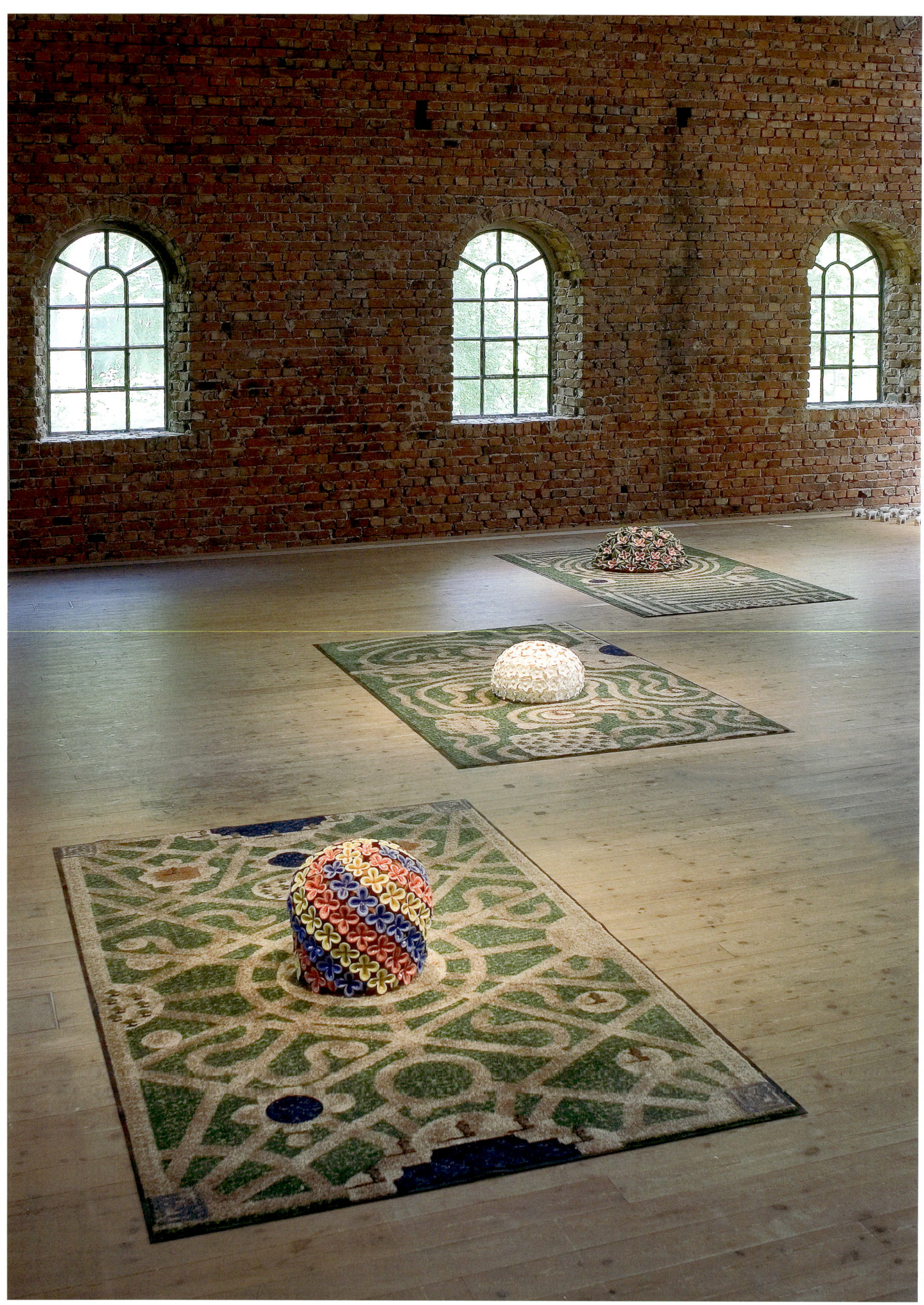

Beauty Bush (2002) and *Privet Ball* (2003) exhibit a keen attention to abstract form and repetition, the vocabulary of high art. To be sure, Dickey's works reference their natural counterparts in their own humorous way, but they are not motivated by the type of anxiety over status that fueled Arneson's practice. Arneson's sarcastic humor is absent in Dickey's work, and replaced by an open, intellectual investigation of the decorative across the larger discipline of sculpture, ceramic sculpture included.

Dickey's 2005 installation *Knots* carried forward her investigation of sculpture's relationship to the decorative and introduced a new theme about the garden as theater—in the artist's words, "a prop in the service of a human fantasy." In *Knots*, spherical terracotta topiaries were mounted on industrial rugs printed with the typical design elements of French gardens, including the rectangular planting bed or *parterre*; the *broderie*, the "embroidered" pattern of clipped hedges within the *parterre*; and the *patte d'oi,* the multiple, tree-lined paths that spread out from a single point in a garden. Dickey has described the *Knots* as representing different experiences of garden landscapes, like stage sets with different themes that the viewer encounters when strolling from one to the other. The tongue-like petals of *Beauty Bush* on the rug titled *Radiate* (2005) referenced the *Garden of Earthly Delights* and its erotic temptations, whereas *Rosebud Bush* on the rug *Lift and Divide* (2005) was an inchoate universe, and *Schneeballen* (2002) on the *Meander* (2005) rug attempted to provide the experience of unadulterated wilderness. In these works, the printed garden plans and their surface punctuation by otherworldly ceramic topiaries highlight the garden as a space of imagination created through the transformation of nature into art.

In her 2007 installation *Cold Pastoral*, Dickey continued her investigation of the garden as a theatrical backdrop. These works derive their forms from sculptural entry points and various types of boundaries used to divide formal gardens into a series of intimate spaces. The installation consisted of eight ceramic works that resemble garden statuary laid out in an *allée* formation, terminating at a mirrored wall that doubled the apparent length of the gallery. Running lengthwise alongside the *allée* was a series of photographs that focus attention on design elements that demarcate space or serve as staging grounds, like the artificial grotto, a popular garden folly. These images were arranged so as to extend the viewer's gaze

Knots, 2005.
Glazed terracotta sculptures on printed industrial rugs, dimensions variable.

Photograph courtesy Skulpturens Hus, Stockholm.

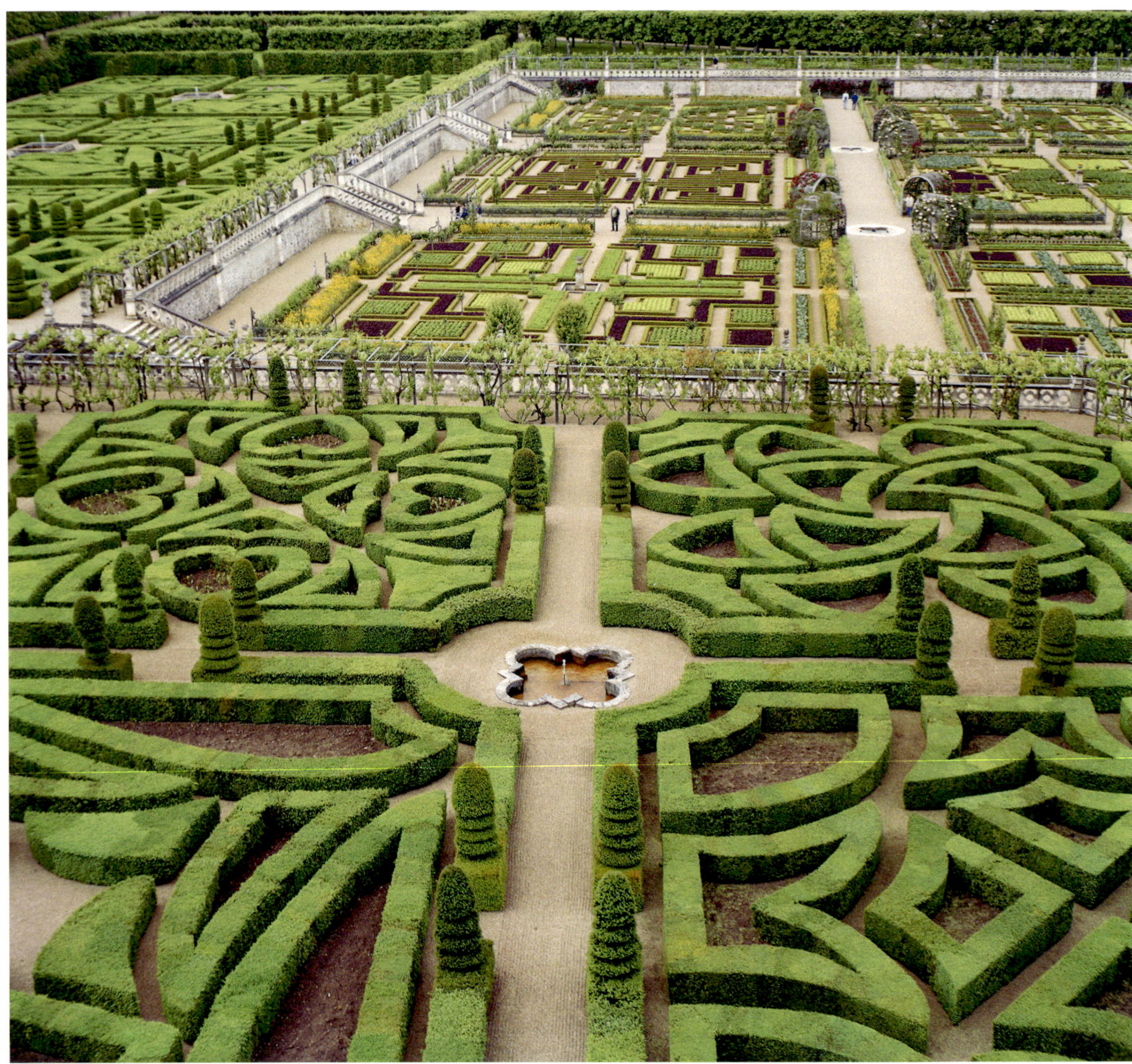

ABOVE

Expanded Field (Villandry), 2007.
Light jet print from 2¼-inch film,
42 × 40 inches.

FACING PAGE

Green Altar, 2007.
Glazed porcelain and cast concrete,
51 × 14 inches.

Box Construction (Villandry), 2007
Light jet print from 2¼-inch film,
36 × 36 inches.

Photograph by Jeff Wells.

beyond the *allée* in the gallery into the larger imaginative space of the garden.

Mirrors and the theme of gardens as spaces of theater or fantasy are also fundamental to Dickey's permanent installation of "bushes" for the Museum of Contemporary Art Denver titled *Museum as Theater as Garden* (2008). The title, as some readers may recognize, is an appropriation of the conceptual artist Dan Graham's "Garden as Theater as Museum," the title of his 1990 essay that examines the history of the garden as a space for sculpture and the appreciation of art, scientific discovery, escape, and amusement.[6] Like museums, gardens were also originally conceived as curated collections with multiple purposes, from cultural preservation to education to leisure.

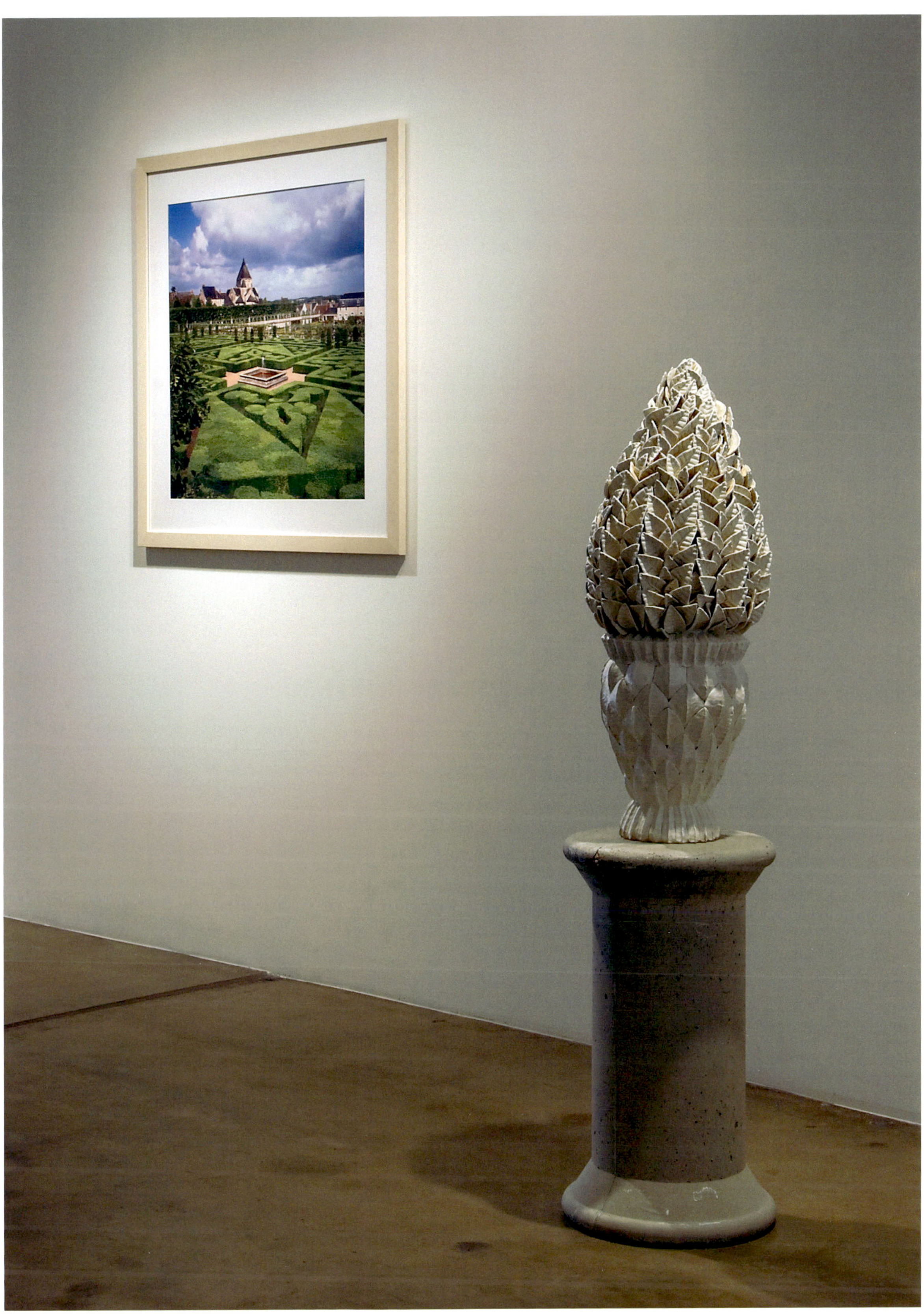

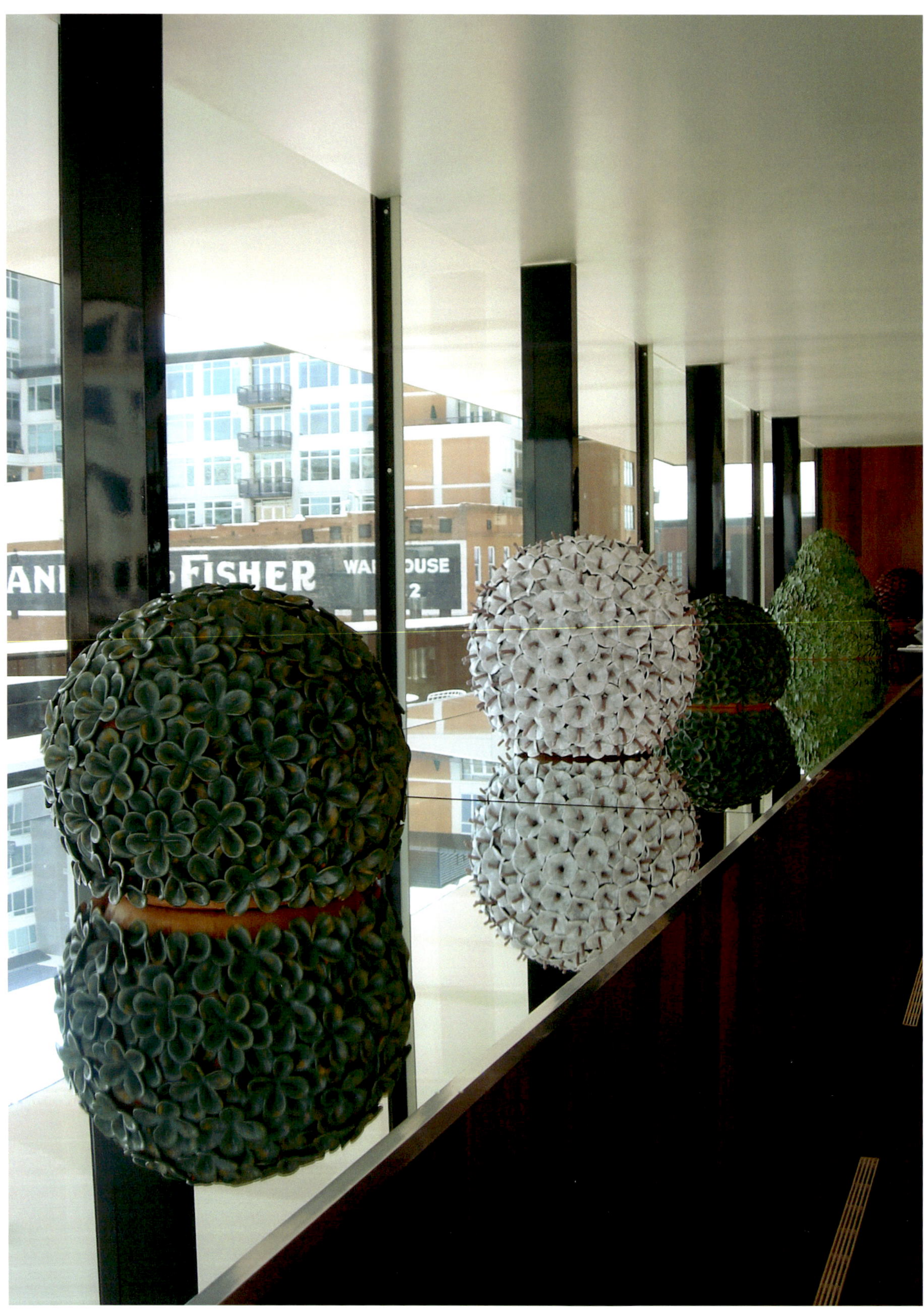
FISHER

Graham's practice as an artist includes the production of a range of architectural forms made for gardens, from pergolas to pavilions to abstract sculptures clad in reflective surfaces that frame, multiply, and compress the viewers' perceptions of themselves and nature, reactivating the historical affiliation of the garden and the museum. For *Museum as Theater as Garden*, Dickey set the "bushes" on a mirrored platform, similarly fracturing and multiplying their forms, and reacquainting us with the museum and the garden as spaces of wonder.

For her installation *All is Leaf* Dickey brought together a series of eight large-scale, geometric forms made of aluminum and clad in green glazed terracotta quatrefoils. The works in this installation, including *Half Arch* (2011), *Corner* (2011), and *Step* (2010), are curious deformations of traditional topiary that toggle between referencing the garden and the art gallery. Accompanying these works were life-size sculptures of animals. Two of them, a hare and a bird of prey, are known inhabitants of gardens. Others, such as the regal lion, more strictly belong to the realm of garden statuary. Like their topiary counterparts, they are also clad in stoneware leaves—in this case white acanthus leaves rather than green quatrefoils. The cladding imbues the animals with a simultaneous and beguiling effect of stoniness and animation, and their placement in relation to the still topiaries set in motion a conversation between the baroque and the minimal. Together they created a magical world, wonderfully evocative of Dickey's stated goal of representing the garden as a site of human fantasy and desire.

Although to some viewers the unusual shapes of the topiaries might simply be a curiosity, others will recognize that the majority of them directly reference Robert Morris's iconic minimalist sculptures from the mid-1960s, such as *Untitled (L Beam)*, *Untitled (Slab)*, and *Untitled (I Beam)*. What was striking about Morris's works was their large-scale, pared-down severity and "installational character."[7] In addition to being huge, simple forms, the works were constructed of humble plywood and painted gray. Their monumental size combined with their lack of surface incident threw viewers' attention outward to the relationship between the sculptures and the surrounding architecture of the gallery.

Although Morris was certainly motivated by spatial concerns and an evolving preference in the art world in this period for oversize, simplified shapes, there was another, less openly discussed force at work and one that is key to understanding Dickey's appropriation of his forms. In an article published in

Museum as Theater as Garden, 2008. Permanent installation of nine glazed terracotta sculptures at MCA Denver.

Photograph courtesy the artist.

2000, Morris described "the great anxiety" for artists of the 1960s over the potential for their work to "fall into the decorative, the feminine, the beautiful, in short, the minor."[8] The way out of this potential fall into décor, according to Morris, was to create sculpture that was "big and heavy," which explains, in part, the scale and severity of his plywood and subsequent minimalist sculptures. In Dickey's *All is Leaf*, nature has claimed these minimalist forms, encasing their surfaces and visually illustrating the tension between art and decoration at the root of modernist aesthetic hierarchies that marginalized ceramics as a lesser, minor practice. The title of the installation, *All is Leaf*, comes from Goethe's *The Metamorphosis of Plants* (1790), in which he discusses the notion of an ideal type underlying natural forms.[9] The idea that minimalist sculpture is a kind of *Urpflanze*, Goethe's name for this archetypal plant, is another example of Dickey's sense of humor when it comes to deflating the heroics of modernist sculpture's claims to purity and autonomy.

Dickey's investigation of the garden at a monumental scale reaches its apex with *Mille-fleur*, a twenty-foot-long freestanding aluminum wall clad in fifteen thousand glazed terracotta quatrefoils. The work's shape recalls a clipped hedge, and on one side of its facade is a colorful composition of hand-painted floral blooms that from a distance creates the illusion of a woven tapestry. Indeed, the title of this work, *Mille-fleur* or "thousand flowers," refers to the allover patterns of flowers or small flowering plants popular in Flemish tapestry. The flowers that cover the surface of this work are drawn specifically from the celebrated fifteenth-century tapestry *The Unicorn in Captivity*, where they surround the unicorn in his gated enclosure, suggesting perhaps that his captivity isn't all bad.

Mille-fleur's illusionistic painting of flowers implies a meadow far more expansive than the edges of its support wall. On its flip side, the continuous surface of green leaves and elemental, border-like form reference the notion of the garden from the opposite perspective, as an enclosure. Dickey's aim of creating "two opposing experiences of landscape in one object—one of the illusion of expansiveness, the other of its presence and containment" embraces a state of "in-betweenness" that departs from the exclusively monochromatic sculptures inspired by minimalism in *All is Leaf*.[10]

The theme of enclosure extends to Dickey's 2015 large-scale installation *Claustrum (Cloister)*. This work, consisting of ten foliate-covered figurative sculptures melding animals and

Inverted L Beam and *I Beam*, 2010 and 2011. Aluminum, glazed terracotta, silicone, and rubber grommets, 46 × 46 × 17 inches (*L Beam*) and 8¼ × 122 × 8¼ inches (*I Beam*).

Photograph by Jeff Wells.

Robert Morris, *Untitled (3 Ls)*, 1965. Painted plywood, 8 × 8 × 2 feet each.

Installation view from Corcoran Gallery of Art, November 24–December 28, 1969. Photo Courtesy Castelli Gallery, New York.

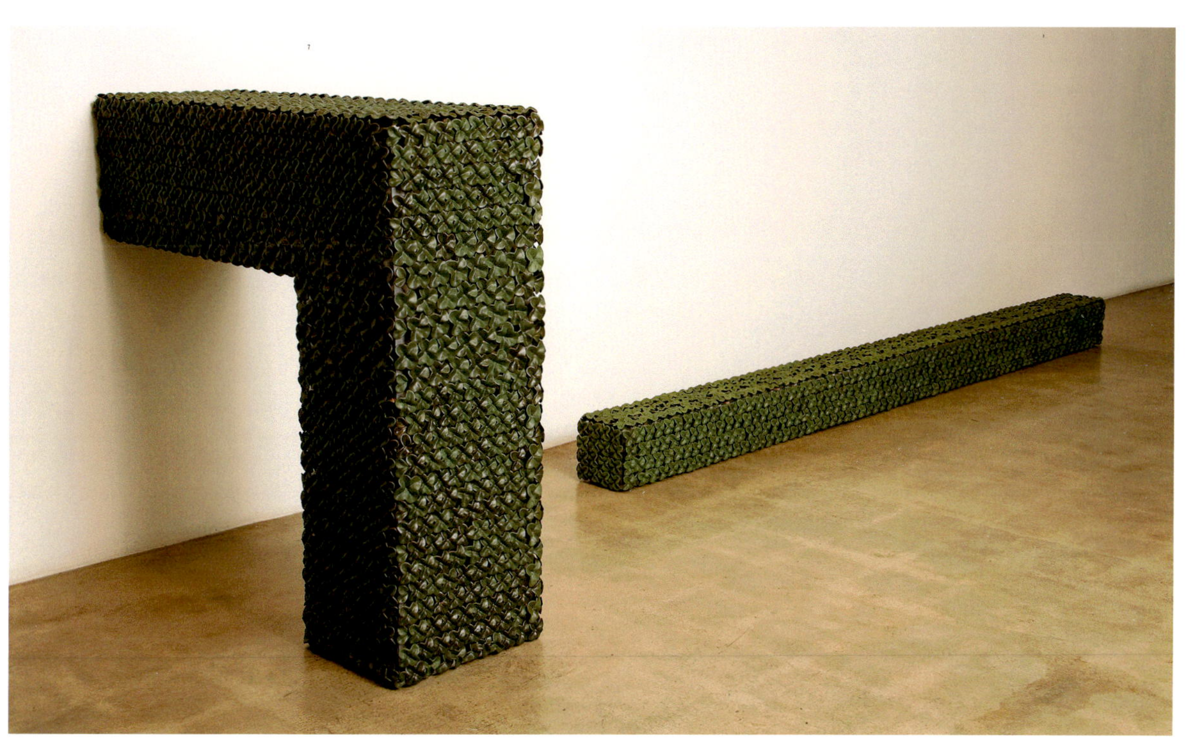

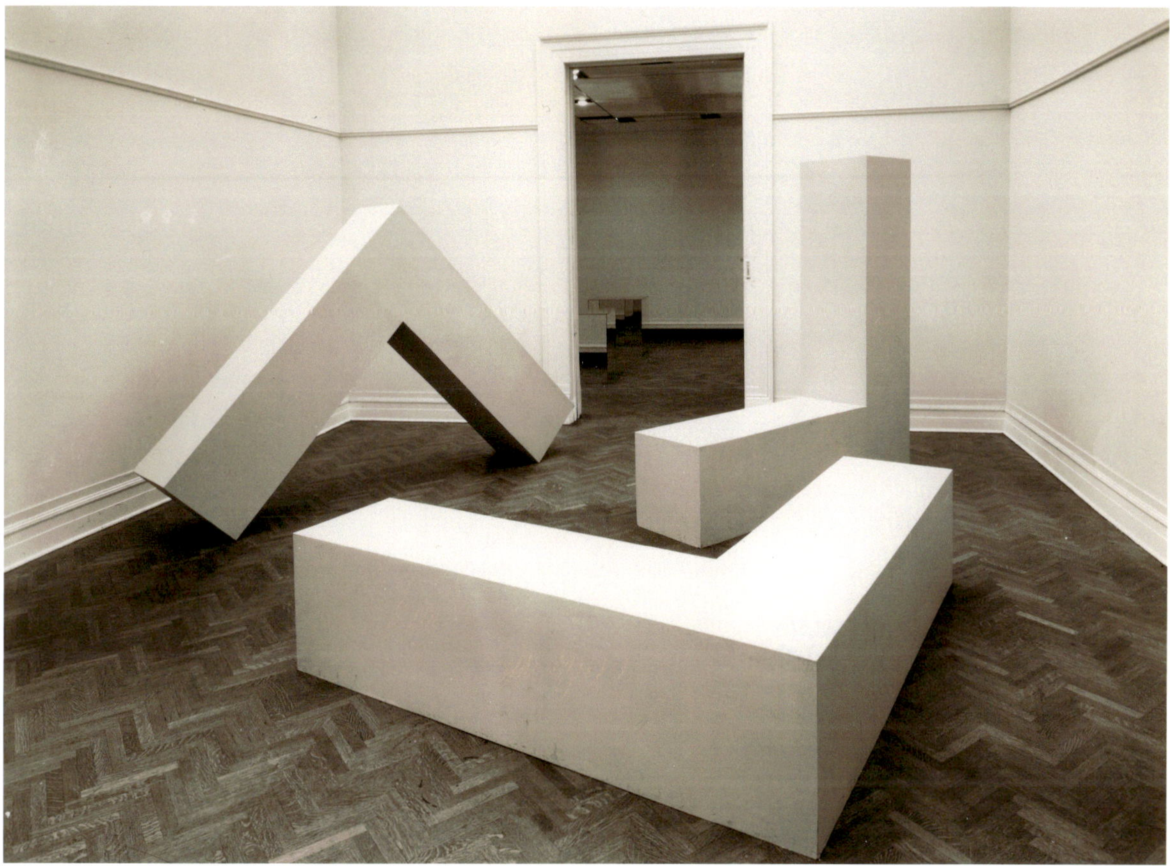

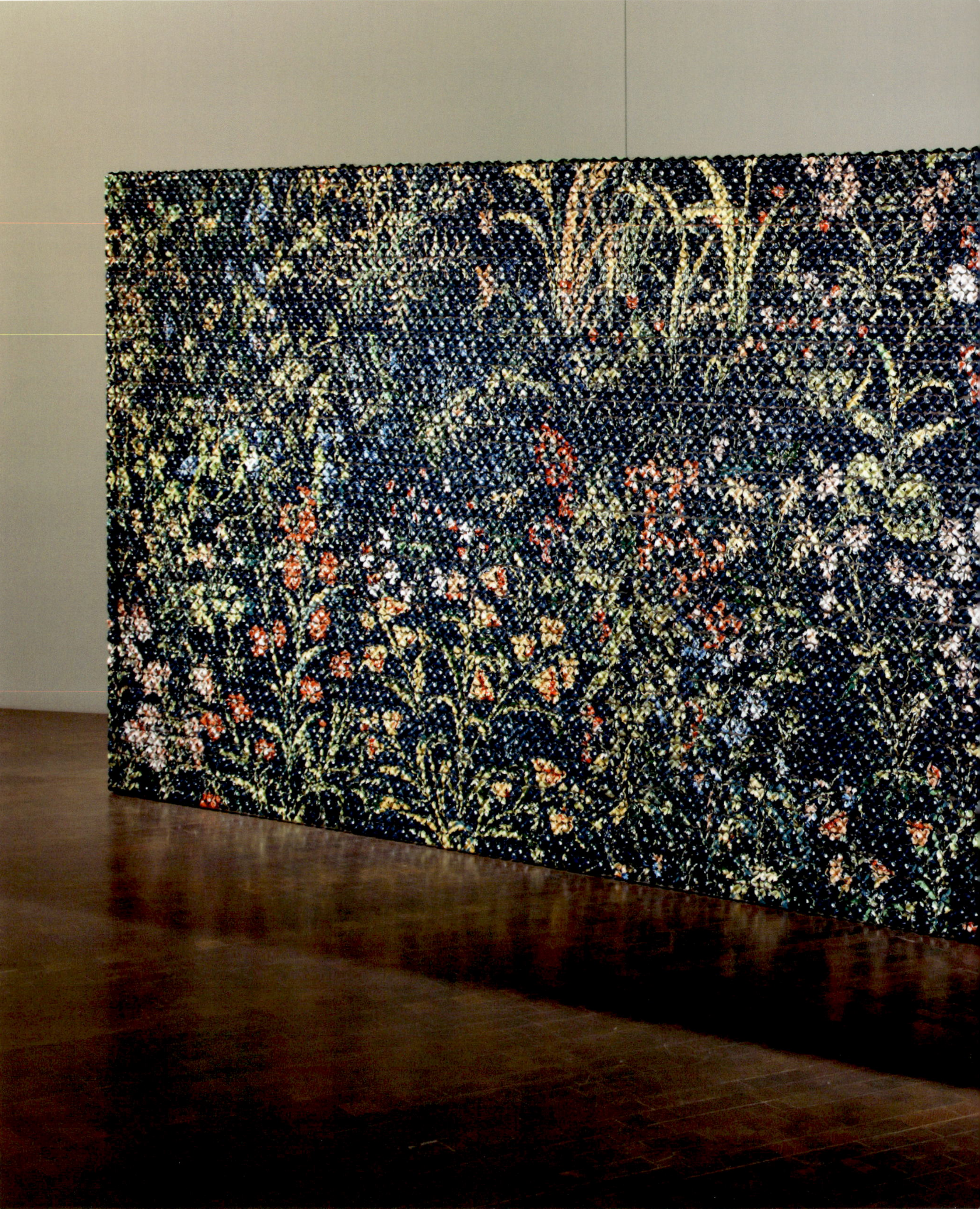

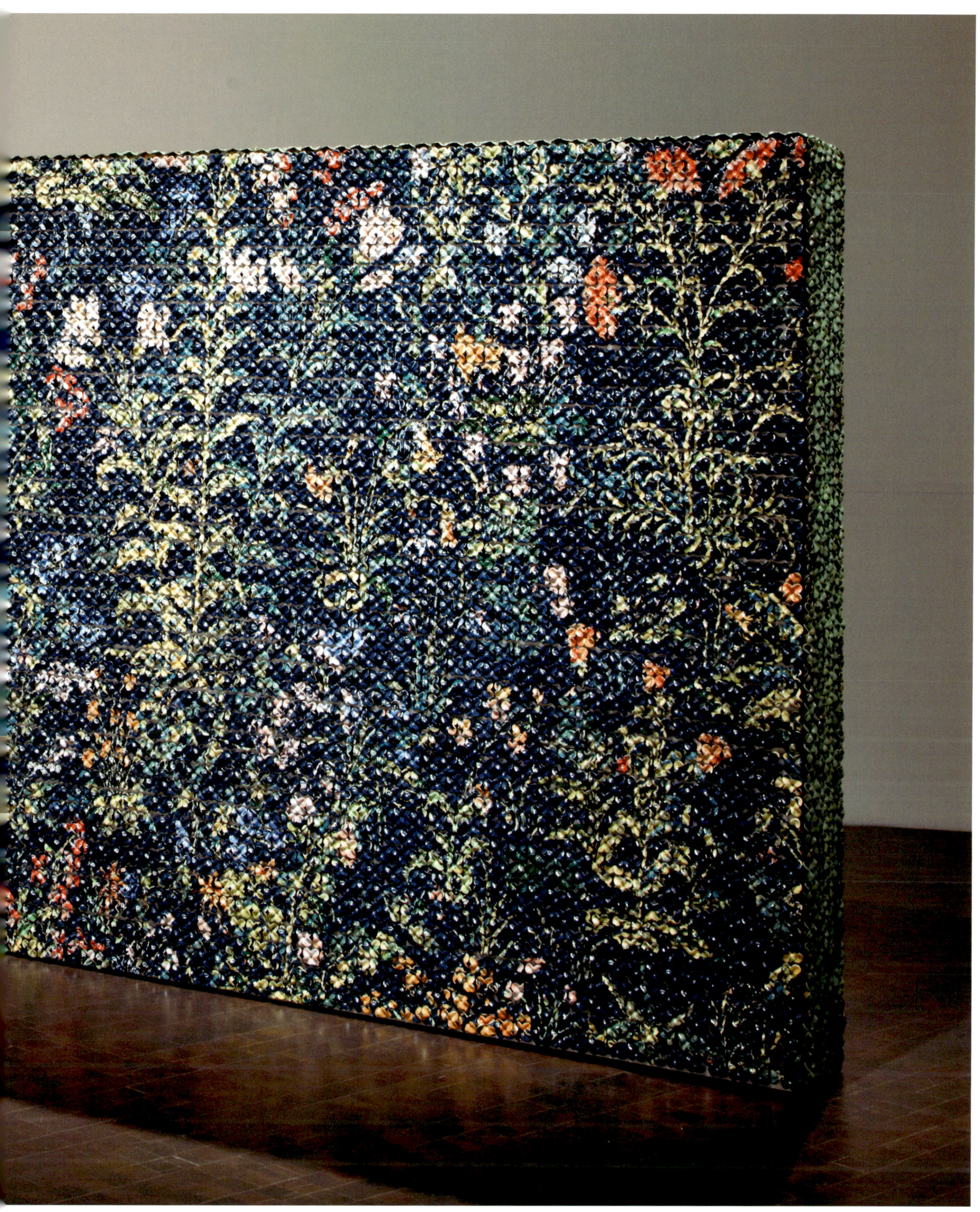

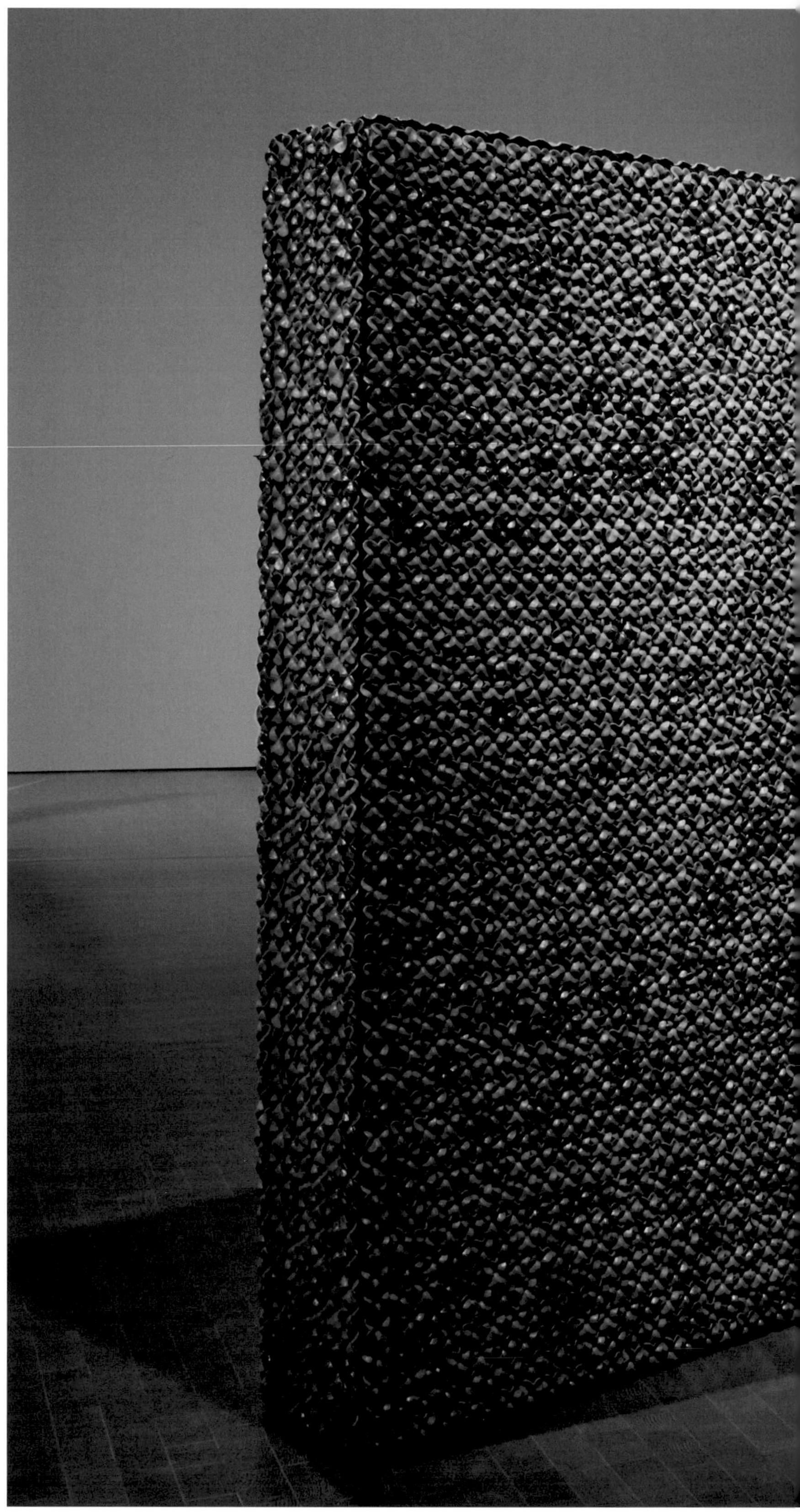

PREVIOUS SPREAD AND RIGHT

Mille-fleur, 2011.
Aluminum, glazed terracotta, rubber grommets, and silicone, 85 × 242 × 15 inches.

Photograph by Jeff Wells, courtesy Denver Art Museum.

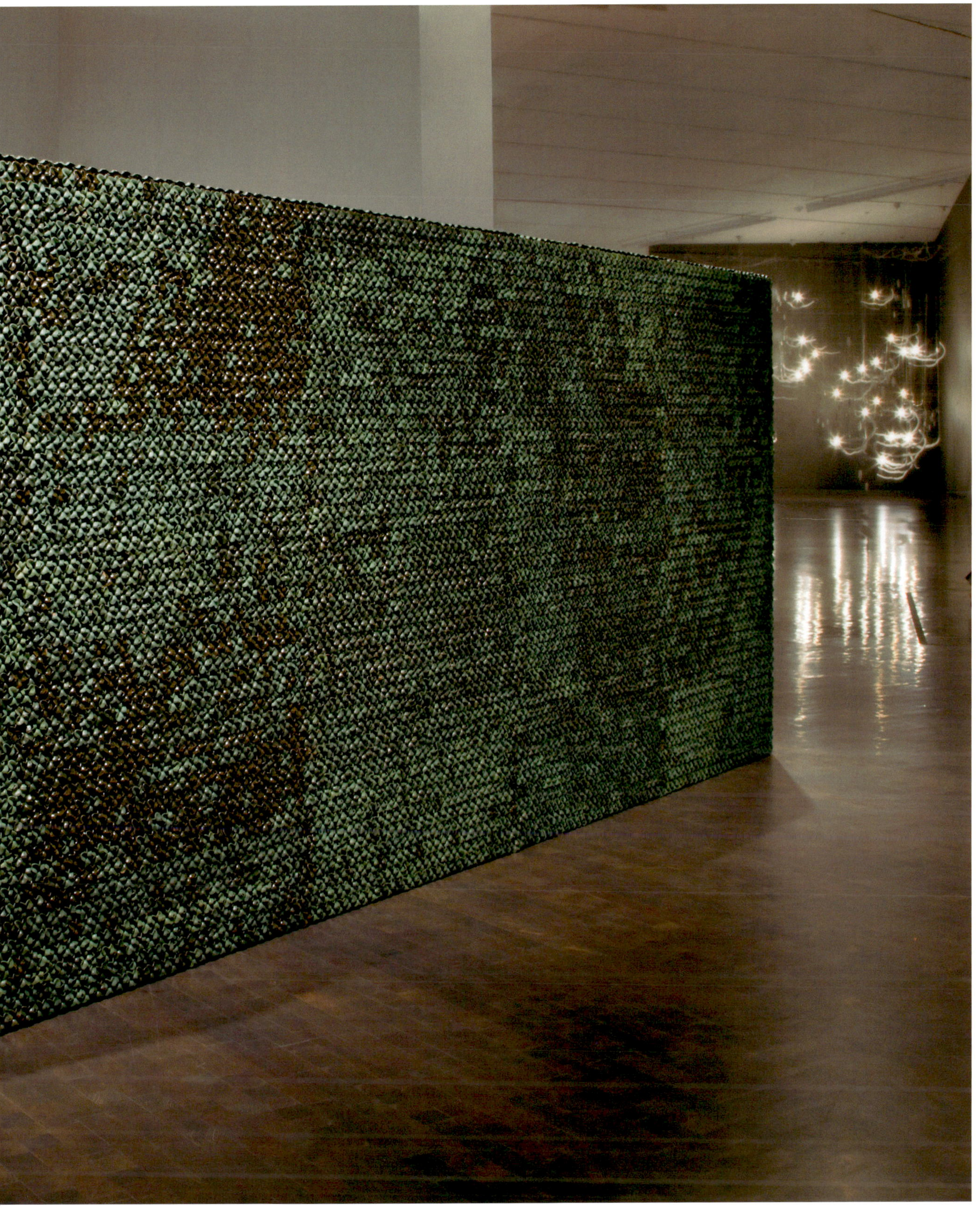

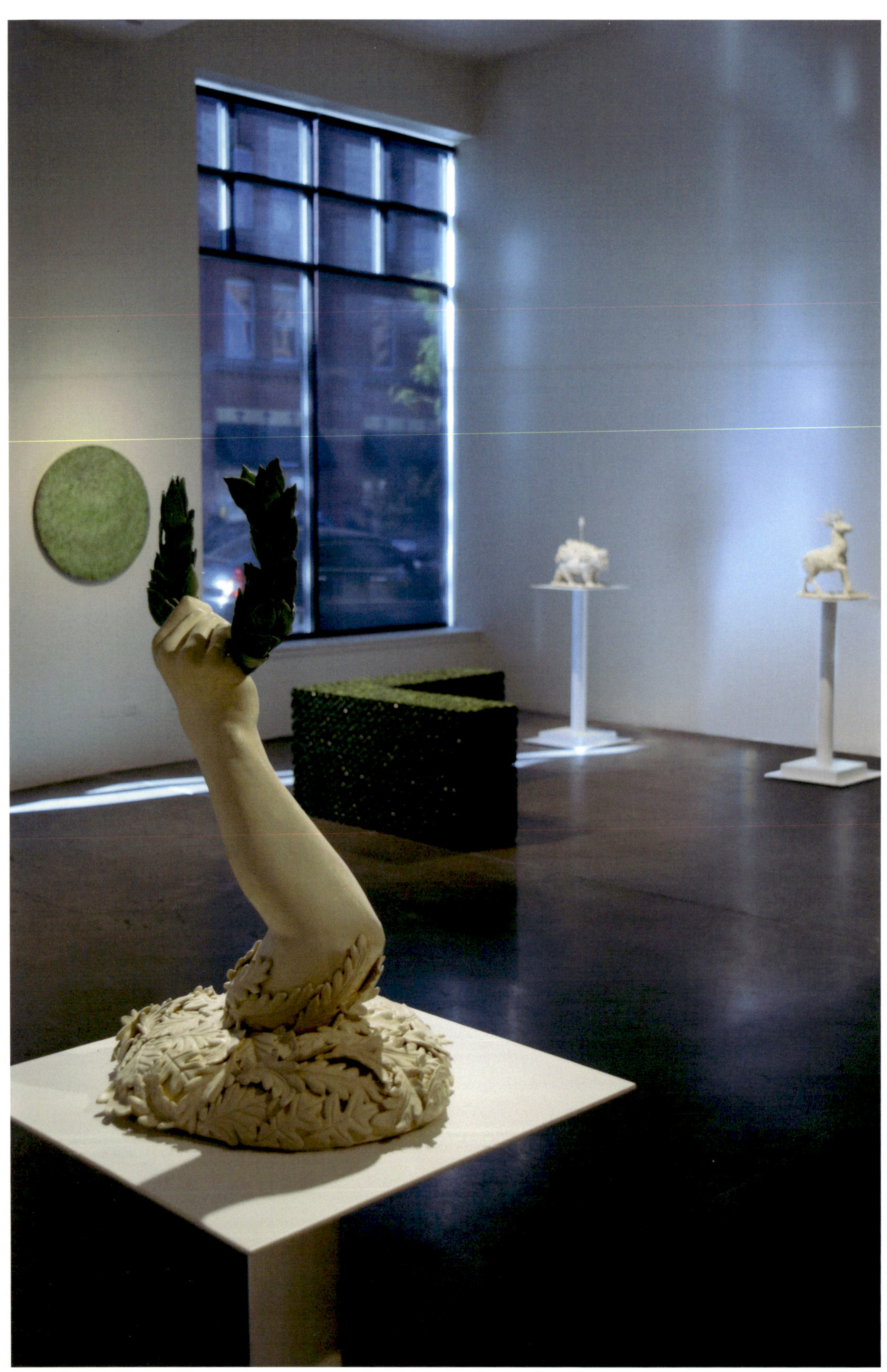

plants into hybrid forms, was inspired by medieval cloister ornamentation. Dickey describes this installation as a "space of consciousness and interiority, like a cloister,"[10] with the ornamentation functioning as an expression of an internal struggle or a representational language in an otherwise silent, closed environment. *Mille-fleur* is simultaneously architecture (a wall or constructed boundary), freestanding sculpture, and illusionistic painting or theatrical screen. The synthesis of these elements conceptually invites the viewer to consider the ways in which the garden is an idealized, immersive field. Whereas nature in that work appears as a decorative element orchestrated and designed for our pleasure, *Claustrum (Cloister)* references a space of quiet supplication shielded from the mundane world. Like the garden, it too is an idealized environment—a contained space—where decorative ornamentation is the stage for an otherworldly experience.

Claustrum (Cloister), installation view, Robischon Gallery, Denver, 2015. Five aluminum wall forms, two terracotta foliate/figurative shrubs, eight foliate figures on powder-coated steel stands, and one sound piece.

Photograph by Jeff Wells.

NOTES

1. In France, Dickey studied and photographed the formal gardens of the Château de Villandry, Vaux-le-Vicomte, Versailles, and Fontainebleau. Dickey also toured Italy, where she concentrated on decorative ceramic styles and traditions.

2. Roland Barthes, "The Reality Effect," in *French Literary Theory Today*, ed. Tzvetan Todorov, trans. R. Carter (Cambridge, England: Cambridge University Press, 1982), 11–17. As quoted by Mimi Hellman, "The Nature of Artifice: French Porcelain Flowers and the Rhetoric of the Garnish," in *The Cultural Aesthetics of Eighteenth-Century Porcelain* (London: Ashgate, 2010), 46.

3. Horace Walpole, as quoted by John Dixon Hunt in *The Genius of the Place: The English Landscape Garden, 1620–1820* (Cambridge, MA: MIT Press, 1988), 11.

4. Robert Arneson as quoted by Glenn Adamson in *Thinking Through Craft* (London: Berg, 2007), 144.

5. Ibid., 143.

6. Dan Graham, "Garden as Theater as Museum," in *Theatergarden Bestiarium: The Garden as Theater as Museum*, ed. Chris Dercon (Cambridge, MA: MIT Press, 1990), 86–105.

7. For an in-depth analysis of Morris's Green Gallery show of 1964 see James Meyer, *Minimalism: Art and Polemics in the Sixties* (New Haven, CT: Yale University Press, 2001), 113–16.

8. Robert Morris, "Size Matters," *Critical Inquiry* 26, no. 3 (Spring 2000): 474–87.

9. Johann Wolfgang von Goethe, *The Metamorphosis of Plants* (1790), with an introduction and photographs by Gordon L. Miller (Cambridge, MA: MIT Press, 2009).

10. Conversation with the artist, May 2016.

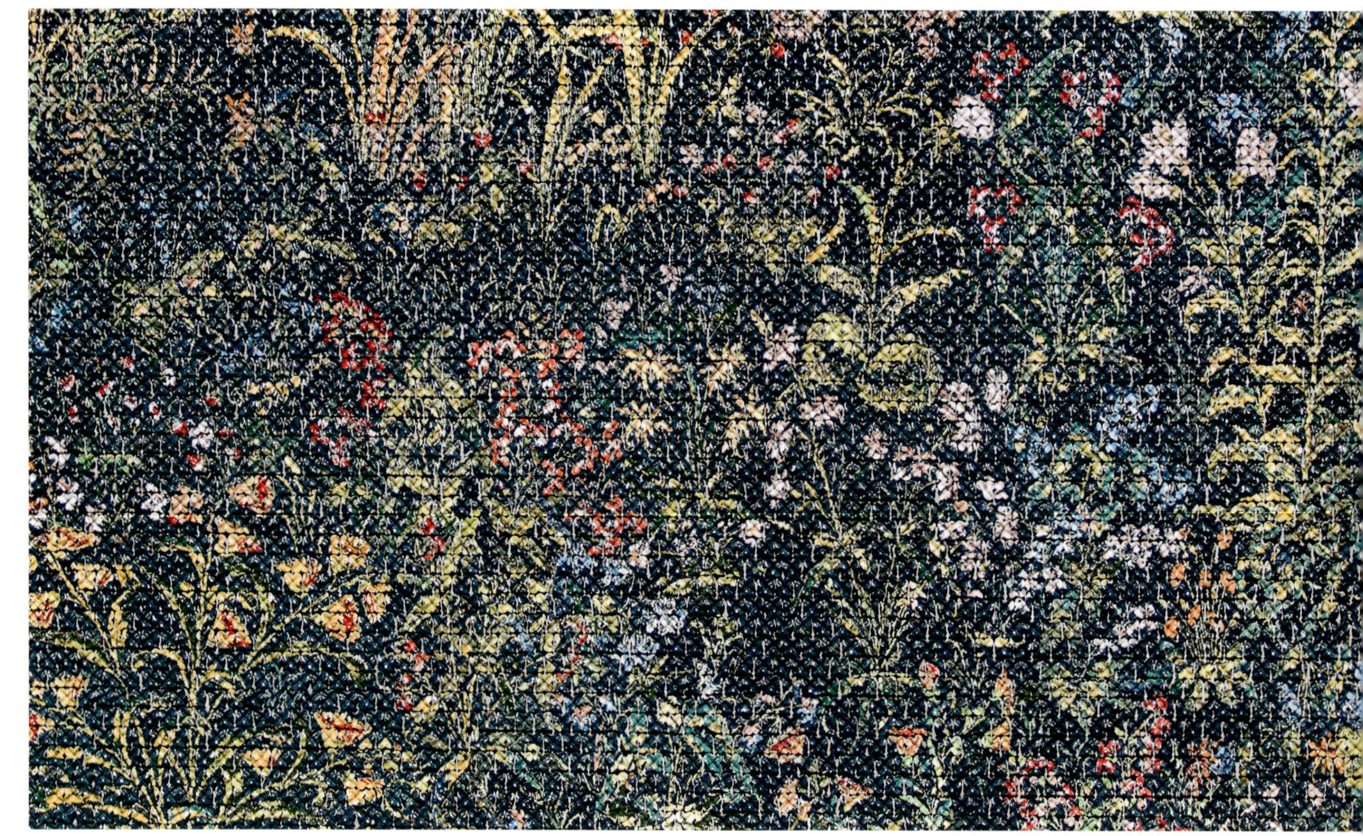

The Mechanics of Kim Dickey's Flowers

Ezra Shales

To introduce Kim Dickey's art by explaining that she works in clay and in floral and vegetal patterns is not untrue, but it begins to paint her into a corner, something words do more harshly than mere sticky pigment. A metaphorical Mack Truck of art historical gibberish bears down on us immediately, clichés about women using floral decoration as vulval/vaginal imagery, or the obsessive-repetitive nature of decorative ornament. This essay aims to flesh out her object matter as separate from her subject matter: the two are different.

Dickey's work shifts in meaning as it responds to sites and alternately stands alone. In one work, her flowers and topiary seem frivolous, in the next they are morbid. Is she engaging sincere allusions to history or wanton postmodern pastiche? I am unsure, and you should be, too. Her twenty-foot-long *Mille-fleur*, composed of fifteen thousand ceramic quatrefoil units precisely mounted on a hedge, dances through history. It is a wall with two faces: one side is a slightly variegated green slab reminiscent of Boston's prudish Grueby pottery from the Arts and Crafts movement circa 1900, while the other evokes an immersive trompe l'oeil Flemish fifteenth-century tapestry. Composed of uniform, precisely made near-mechanical units, the hedge speaks to museological time and to contemporary pixelation—both/and, not either/or. In a way, Dickey's large scaffolding covered with flowers does harken back to Grueby, where scores of women were hired to add buds, ferns, and garlands to the vases that men had made. But another visual logic lies closer at hand. I imagine her, a fellow New Yorker, entranced by the unicorn tapestries in the Metropolitan Museum of Art's Cloisters, and also transforming Robert Morris's gray slabs and somber plinths into something more delicate and deliciously tactile. Perhaps these flowers are made by a closeted admirer of Jonathan Adler's cloyingly cute retro boutiques, revivalist Marimekko, or Andy Warhol's enormous deadpan hibiscuses from 1964.

A flower can embody the insipid or the divine. Blossoms can give life but also can kill—"Either that wallpaper goes or I do," Oscar Wilde supposedly opined on his deathbed. In fact, Wilde actually declared, "This wallpaper and I are fighting a duel to the death"—a most succinct description of the human drive to reconcile the flame of individual perception and the material world against which it burns. A blossoming bud does not *always* do anything: sometimes it signals temporal constraints, vanity, and at others it seems to connote eternal vitality. Flowers have a particularity one second, and the next speak

Mille-fleur (detail), 2011.
Aluminum, glazed terracotta, silicone, and rubber grommets, 85 × 242 × 15 inches.

Crystal Bridges Museum of American Art, Bentonville, Arkansas, 2015.6. Photograph by Marc F. Henning.

in large generalizations—of national style, religion, cultural zeitgeist. Look at the flowers in the Blue Mosque in Mazar-e-Sharif, Afghanistan, or the roses on the walls, floors, and chairs of London's Houses of Parliament to apprehend these larger forces driving forth petal, pistil, and stamen.

Criticism has cunningly deflowered flowers—a good thing to avoid. As made clear by works such as Robert Arneson's *Gold Lustered Rose* (1966) and Eugene Von Bruenchenhein's *Untitled (Flower)* (ca. 1960), flowers are a mystical and never-ending resource for artists, and they have no singular meaning. Arneson might have been skewering amateurism or lamenting the status of ceramics in the art world, but he made something beautiful and large enough to stick one's head into: to simply see it as scale, color, and form is to lose sight of those things and realize that he understood—manually and perhaps emotionally—that a two-foot flower has a pretty large bouquet; it holds a room. Von Bruenchenhein redeems the categorization of the amateur and reveals such a label as revolting elitist claptrap: his tender blossom proves that there is always reason and room for more vulnerability and fragility in our world. The proximity of time during which they made these flowers also suggests the uselessness of decades and isms to define floral symbolism. For a serious artist, as for a child, it's always worthwhile to fashion a rose.

A most famous misreading of flowers occurred with Georgia O'Keeffe and her paintings: a century of programmatic psychological interpretation mistook petals for pussy. But if her individual biography gets removed—if we don't know Alfred Stieglitz's nude portraits of her, and that he abandoned his family for her, and we don't sense his off-screen erection—her flower power (and other botanic representations) resemble something more collective and cranial.[1] "I made you take time to look at what I saw and when you took time to really notice my flower you hung all your own associations with flowers on my flower and you write about my flower as if I think and see what you think and see of the flower—and I don't," confessed O'Keeffe in a 1939 catalogue for Stieglitz's gallery.[2] If the sex drive in plant life produces flowers, it is neither gender nor copulation that makes for beautiful representations of blooming blossoms. O'Keeffe's jack-in-the-pulpit series of six paintings from 1930 is like a photographic staccato—a shortening of the focal length—and also an exploration of abstraction.

Some of Kim Dickey's works touch on formalism and simultaneously suggest a subtext of deeper, intimate, and more

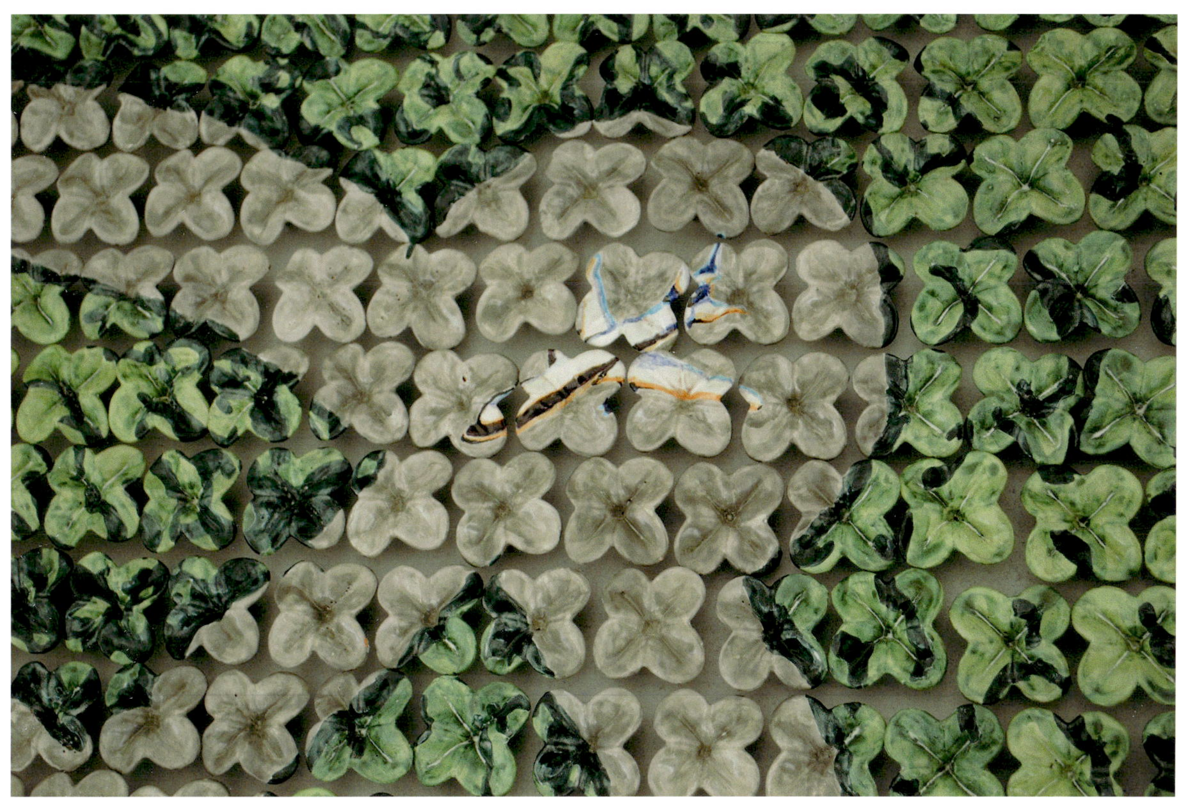

Parterre (detail), 2012.
Aluminum, glazed terracotta, silicone, and rubber grommets, 15 × 15 × 1¾ feet.

Photograph courtesy the artist.

subjective meanings. *Parterre* (2012), a shin-high fifteen-square-foot miniature garden maze, plays with aerial views and rigid symmetries, and evokes not the content of O'Keeffe's jack-in-the-pulpit series but her method. In *Parterre*, Dickey's glazed terra-cotta flowers are photomechanical and also abstract, and the total effect is most legible from afar. It shows a garden somewhere but also nowhere. Offering a fragmentary vista, it speaks to a state of placelessness—appropriately, it was in fact a commission for Denver International Airport. Do we entertain this fragment of the picturesque as a vacation destination, idealized cultural pilgrimage, or childhood memory? It occupies a strange pictorial space that is neither physically assertive nor accessible as a tactile field. If Dickey is toying with the minimalist anti-monument in *Mille-fleur*, *Parterre* is more acutely asserting that we cannot enter the illusion of her verdant fields.

"It went through a whole cycle of art history: the primitive, the archaic, the classic, and then on to the baroque.... All those stages were interesting and complete in themselves, but just not what the final version was or what I intended," noted Jay DeFeo when describing *The Rose* (1958–66).[3] A single painting that weighs more than one ton, *The Rose* is another monolithic

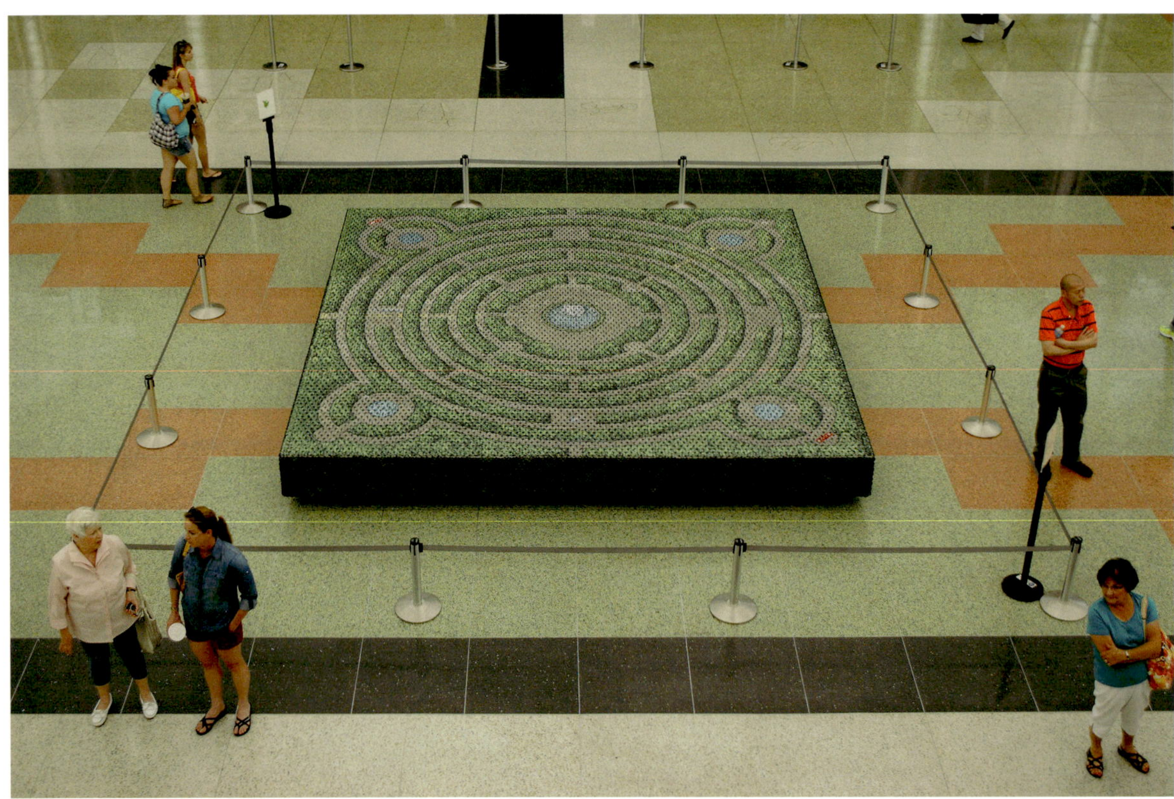

ABOVE AND FACING PAGE

Parterre, installation view, Great Hall, Jeppesen Terminal, Denver International Airport, 2012. Aluminum, glazed terracotta, silicone, and rubber grommets, 15 × 15 × 1¾ feet.

Photograph courtesy the artist.

flower from art history that has been hermeneutically teased and tortured. Once again, no movements help to unlock interpretation. Its earlier name, *Deathrose*, should unnerve certainty. The image is legible as geometry and light; it is not representational, yet hardly abstract. It is a monumental object that has a weighty, rough-hewn presence. It is more wall than painting, and certainly an anti-illusion. In the late 1990s a curator recovered this semi-flower and declared it a semaphore. Sealed inside a wall in the San Francisco Art Institute for twenty years, DeFeo's never-finished process-oriented work came to symbolize the failure of the feminist movement to change the art game. It had not been exhibited since 1969, and DeFeo left no interpretations of it. Scholars have suggested that its meaning might lie in Kabbalah mysticism, or perhaps Christian theology, surrealism, or Sufi poetry, but recently Anne Wilkes Tucker probed the immense photographic oeuvre that DeFeo left and noted that flowers were an ongoing concern, as a formal and visual language, not necessarily specific symbols.[4] Dickey's *Mille-fleur* might have the same temporal spin through ancient tapestry, rococo garden landscape, and the hedges of the modern suburban McMansion. Flowers

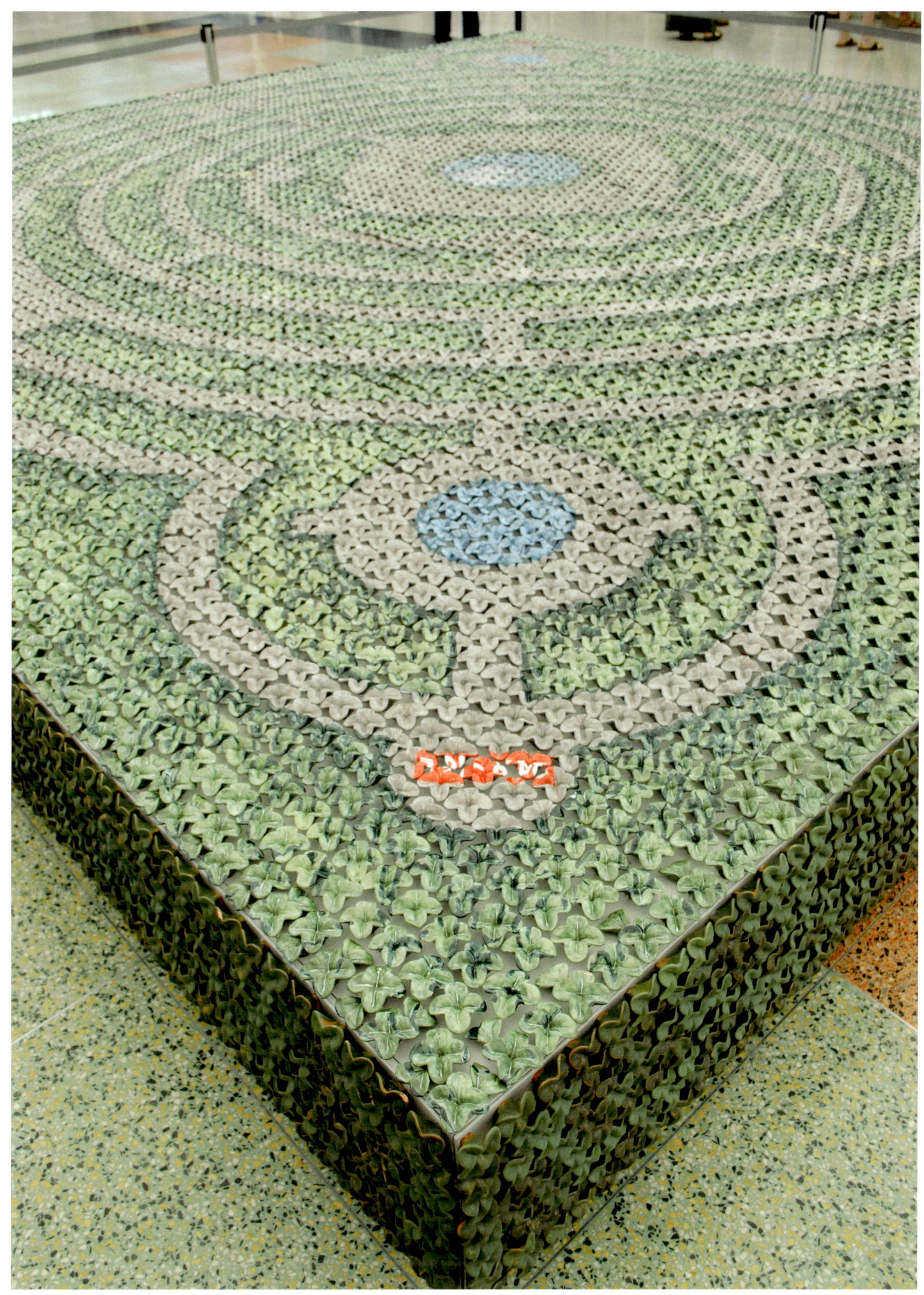

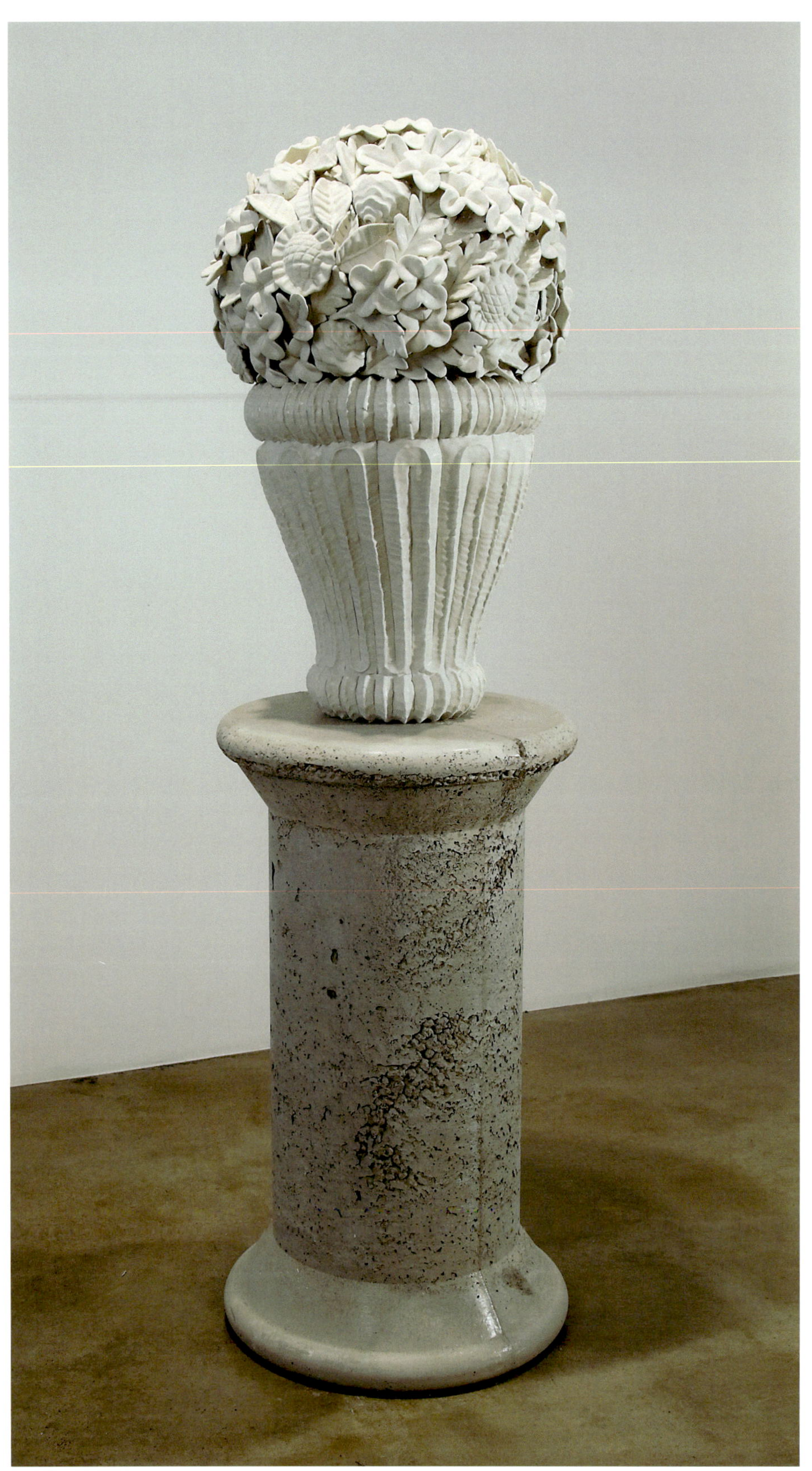

have a potent, innate desire to construct a lineage—they are designed for self-preservation—but as art they have been interpreted and deconstructed to suit strange genealogies, whether an auctioneer or art dealer's market value or an art historian's ideological program.

In her layers of historical allusion, joyful abandon, and monumental ambition, Dickey builds on the legacy of Betty Woodman more than the brutal sarcasm and parody of Arneson. Kim Dickey's flowers are restless, a *pas de deux* with the antique and our very own era of manicured golf courses amid drought-addled deserts. Flowers are good to think with and they offer two certainties: their generative capacity is without limits, and when we pass by one in bloom, we usually stop to take a closer look.

NOTES

1. O'Keeffe willingly transformed her body and self into a spectacular image. She was reticent to conduct interviews with scholars but always willing to pose for a professional photographer. See Wanda Corn, "Telling Tales: Georgia O'Keeffe on Georgia O'Keeffe," *American Art* 23, no. 2 (Summer 2009): 54.

2. Rita Donagh, "Georgia O'Keeffe in Context," *Oxford Art Journal* 3, no. 1, "Women in Art" issue (April 1980): 46.

3. DeFeo to Rebecca Solnit in Bill Berkson, "The Romance of The Rose," in *Jay DeFeo: Selected Works 1952–1989*, ed. Constance Lewallen (Philadelphia: Moore College of Art and Design, 1996), 26.

4. Anne Wilkes Tucker, "When a Plant Is Not a Plant: The Botanical Photographs of Jay DeFeo," *Aperture*, no. 186 (Spring 2007): 30–35.

Bouquet, 2007.
Glazed stoneware and concrete,
49 × 15 inches.

Photograph by Jeff Wells.

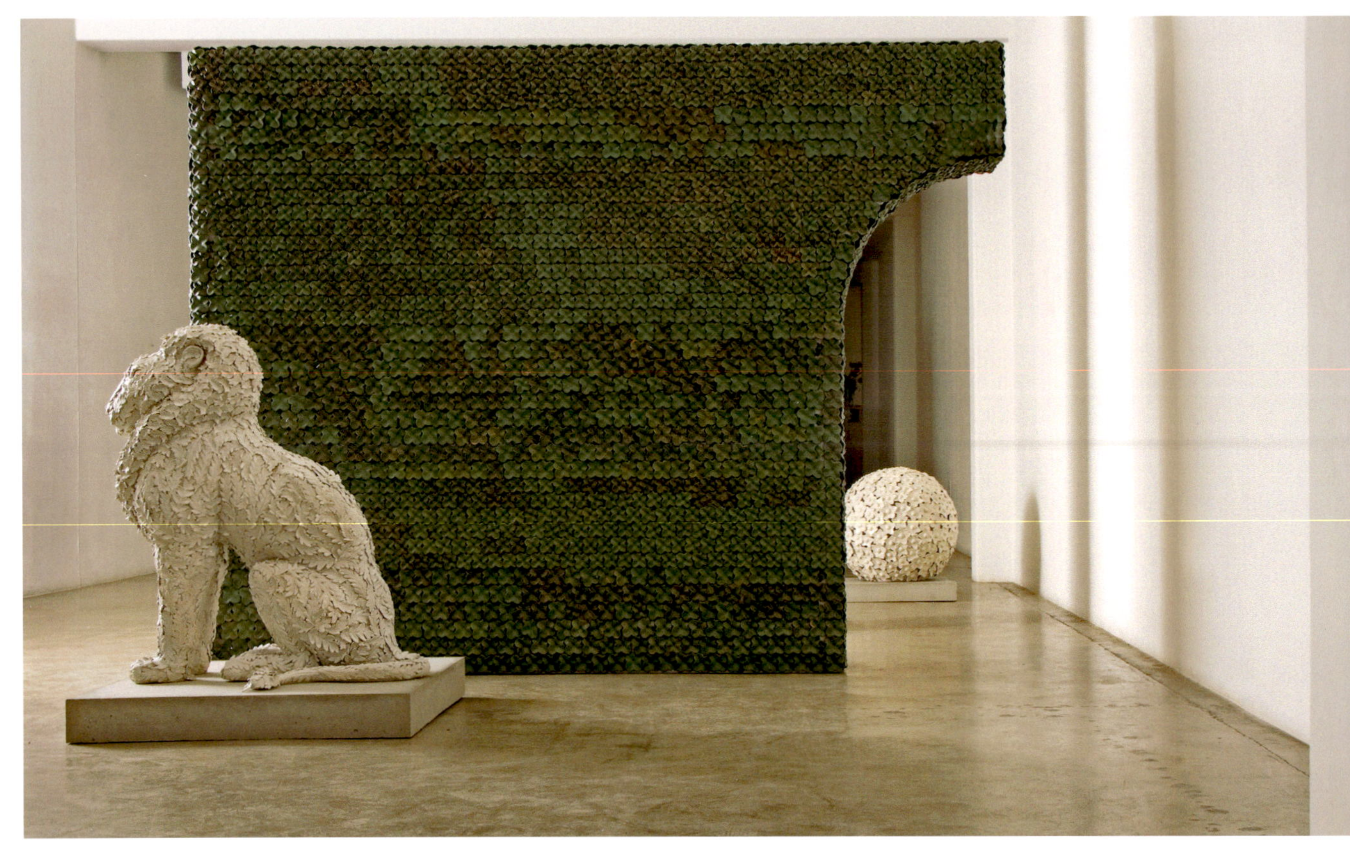

Interview with the Artist

Nora Burnett Abrams

Nora Burnett Abrams Let's jump right in, Kim. What were your earliest creative works? Were you working in sculpture from the beginning?

Kim Dickey When I was very young, I was constantly drawing and painting. My earliest drawings were botanical illustrations, and landscapes.

NBA Were you drawing from books, or from actual gardens?

KD From the garden, and surrounding countryside, and my imagination.

NBA Did you have any kind of artist role models when you were growing up?

KD Although I never met her, my great aunt, Margaret Redmond, was a professional artist with a studio on Newbury Street in Boston from the turn of the century through the 1940s. She designed stained glass windows throughout the Northeast including a rose window for Trinity Church. I grew up with her paintings and drawings in our childhood home. We also had many art books at home and I would pore over them again and again. I was fascinated by Hieronymus Bosch and Bruegel, among others.

My mother was a self-taught artist. She painted, drew, wrote, and was deeply involved in landscape design—gardening, specifically—and took me to New York City to the Met and MoMA many times as a child. So, I grew up in a family with a reverence for art and I recognized that making art was a rewarding path early on. There was a joy I experienced in my art classes that was unique. While the academics I was pursuing were deeply engaging intellectually, studying art offered a different level of understanding and knowledge and emotional content to me.

NBA When did you first encounter ceramics as a medium?

KD I was in the sixth grade. I was so taken by the material, so transformed by the experience of working with it, that every time I came out of the class people would stop me in the hall and remark at how my demeanor had changed. I was glowing. I truly fell in love with it. I didn't take another ceramics class until quite a few years later, and then had the exact same experience. There was an incredibly visceral, physical connection, and an emotional connection that was profound.

Wolfgang's Lion and *Half Arch* from *All is Leaf*, 2011.
Glazed stoneware on concrete, 39 × 32 × 32 inches (*Wolfgang's Lion*), and aluminum, glazed terracotta, silicone, and rubber grommets, 73 × 98 × 14 inches (*Half Arch*).

Photograph by Jeff Wells.

I think I was lucky to have stumbled on it, and then to have recognized that it was indeed the right material for me. There were times when I questioned the specific disciplinary choice, primarily out of not wanting to limit my exploration as an artist. In the early 1980s, ceramics was not as sexy as it is today, or as widely embraced by the art world. Back then, Julian Schnabel was hitting it big, and Jeff Koons.

NBA It was an era of big, heroic painting and sculpture.

KD So while I knew that ceramics was potentially fraught as an arena within the contemporary art world, it offered room, off the radar perhaps, to challenge traditional assumptions about the medium. There were still a lot of hang-ups about it, and possibly prejudices against it as a material, particularly given its connection to craft, but I never bought into that.

NBA I imagine many of those prejudices still remain, and you still fight against them—the relation of ceramics to domestic objects, for instance.

KD Perceptions about the material, negative or positive never stopped me from working with it or finding it to be a rich conceptual arena to explore. However, there was a time when anything to do with utility used to be viewed as compromising art or pure artistic inquiry. But my generation (and many artists before us, like Fluxus, the Gutai group, Franz West) came up questioning those criteria, and challenged them. Physical interaction, engagement in role playing, engagement in theatrical touch, and so on started to be embraced. Then that opened up the possibility of objects of use also being seen less as solely utilitarian or at the service of a strict design function.

Not only were art-world boundaries starting to loosen with so many more varied interpretations and criteria in terms of what constituted art practices, but the design world also started blurring the boundaries between application and form.

NBA And design simply became a lot more popular. But these prejudices we're speaking of within the contemporary art world against craft or objects of use—I believe you started to mine these early on, deliberately. You found an arena where you could do both: make objects to be used and that also had a conceptual underpinning. I'm thinking of some of the earliest objects that are in the exhibition.

Lady J (Cornea #2), 1996.
Porcelain, 3 × 6½ × 2¼ inches.

Photograph courtesy the artist.

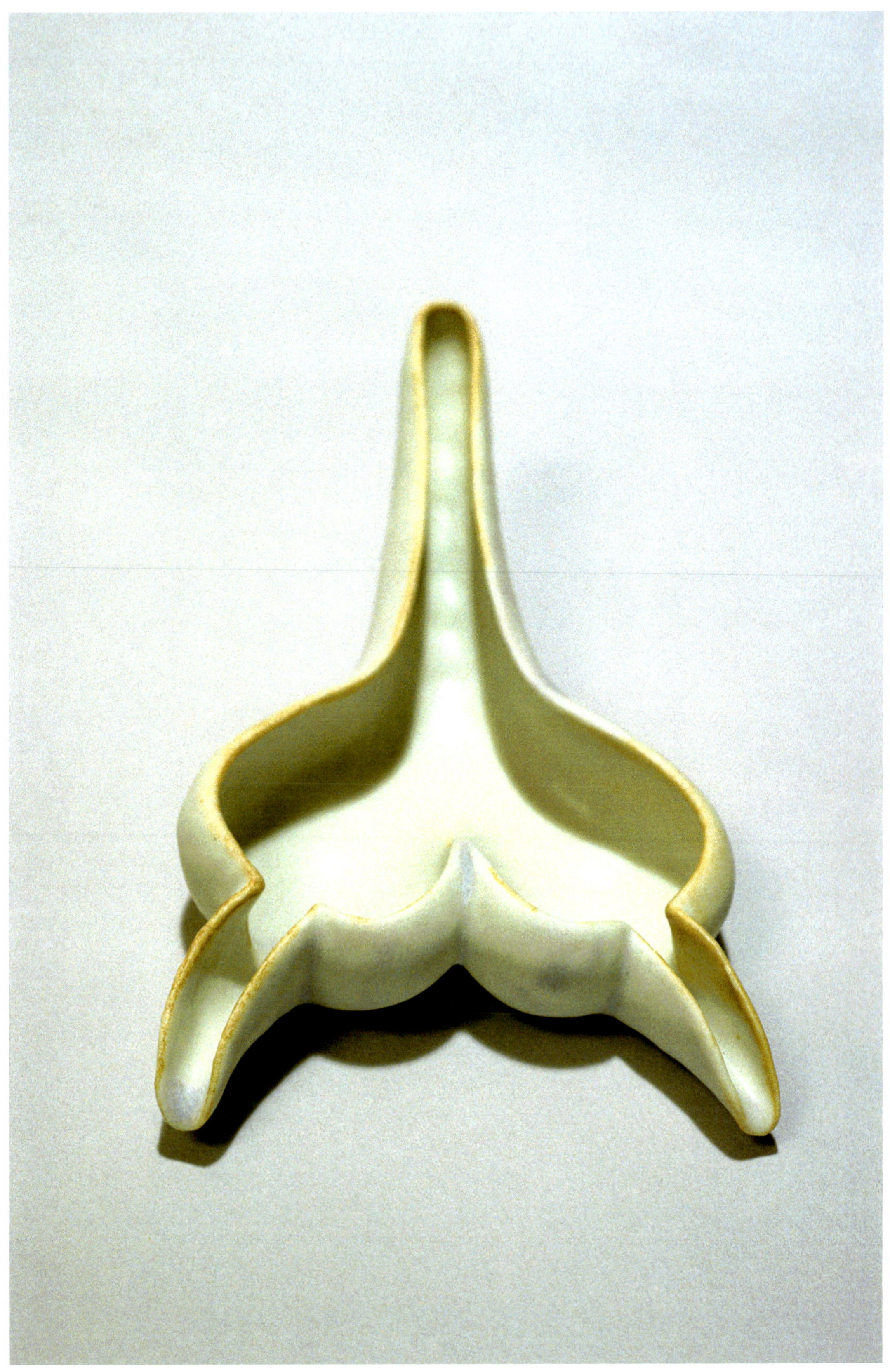

KD The *Lady Js*, and even *The Fall Set*. What I realized about object making is that it is inherently theatrical—that all sculpture is theatrical.

NBA Museums are theatrical places.

KD Exactly. Even gardens are theater. It gave me this wonderful perspective on how you could re-envision or even recontextualize the role of the object and the role of object-maker. Then, importantly, I came across the Objectivist poets: Louis Zukofsky, Charles Simic, Jean Follain, and Francis Ponge. These were French and American poets working in the 1940s, 1950s, and 1960s. Part of their project was to replace the object as subject. By this I mean, to see the world around you as playing a critical role. That question took hold in me: how could an object both be the setting and a character?

I'm certain that living in New York after graduate school helped me question what's inside and what's outside. I was populating my studio with a lush environment of my own creation. This idea emerged for me that the object could extend into the environment, become the environment, and then we could recognize ourselves as objects in that environment. If we suddenly see objects as subjects, we connect ourselves to these things in a much more conscious way. There's a sort of extension of responsibility that potentially happens.

NBA The way you're speaking about the environment and objects in relation to the environment—was that thinking based on your studies of landscape and landscape architecture as an undergraduate?

KD Yes, but it goes back even earlier, in part from witnessing my mother's passion for gardening, and the commitment and joy she exuded while building these sites around our home. But what interested me was landscape history, and linking the history to certain repeated forms, and where they come from—their origins. So, while at Rhode Island School of Design I studied the formal design of the Paradise garden, tracing that through ancient literature: the Song of Songs, Dante, and Boccaccio. What did it look like? Finding that there were certain kinds of echoes to every discussion of Paradise, I realized that gardening was an activity of trying to attain the ideal. What's this relationship between the real and the ideal, the imaginary places that only exist in one's imagination and our need or desire, perhaps *my* need or desire, to construct those things in the flesh?

The garden addresses this human condition, and this between-ness that I'm speaking of between the real and the ideal. Where do you find the space to dream, and then try to construct it? This space connected to the house, but touching the edge of an outside wilderness, within the private domain, not unadulterated nature but a construct, a theater of your own design—it became a charged place to engage many of my questions.

NBA Given that you were living in the concrete jungle—a densely urban, architecturally crowded city—how were you thinking about the garden or landscape in relation to your immediate context?

KD I've always been fascinated by the *hortus conclusus*, which is the enclosed, walled garden. The wall, the boundary line, as well as the enclosure, are not only real experiences of urban life, but also very much embedded in notions of vessel making or enclosing volumes. The city offered a wonderful opportunity for me to investigate the notion of the cloister, meaning a garden within an architectural framework, a site of sanctuary that is completely interior, completely enclosed and shut to the outside world. My studio has always been that—a place to examine my own nature.

NBA You were emerging in the late 1980s, in a moment of postmodernism that basically sanctioned everything.

KD Pluralism, certainly.

NBA And the sense that nothing is more rarified than anything else, that everything, in terms of both material and subject of art, is open. But even still, for someone coming from a craft-based tradition, it takes a lot of effort to get credibility, access support, both critical and financial. You had to pioneer a tricky and, frankly, uncharted course in order to maintain the integrity of the medium that you were dedicated to, and also assert its conceptual value beyond its possible functional value. Did you think about it in such binary terms at the time?

KD I was well aware of the difficulty of the path that I was choosing.

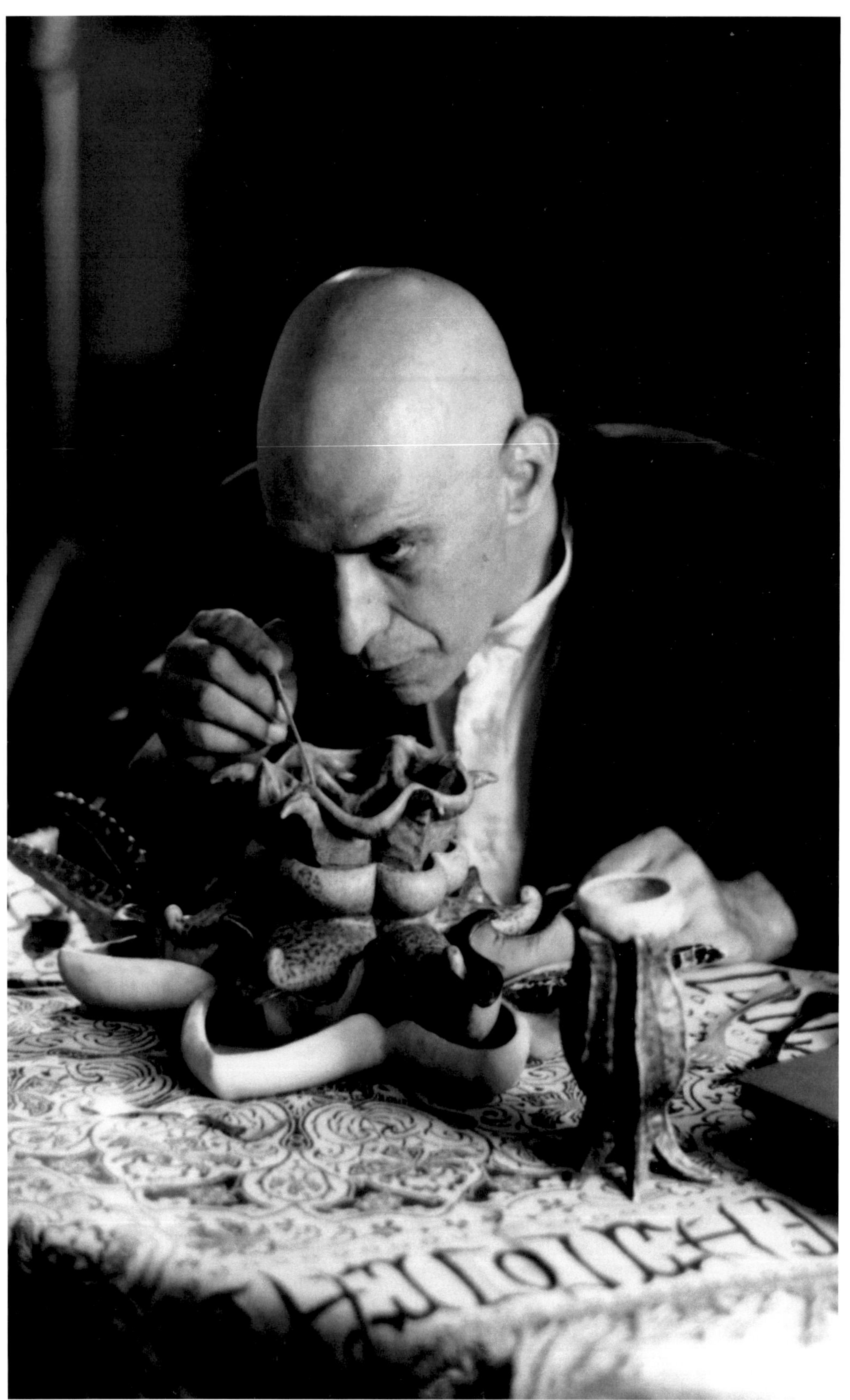

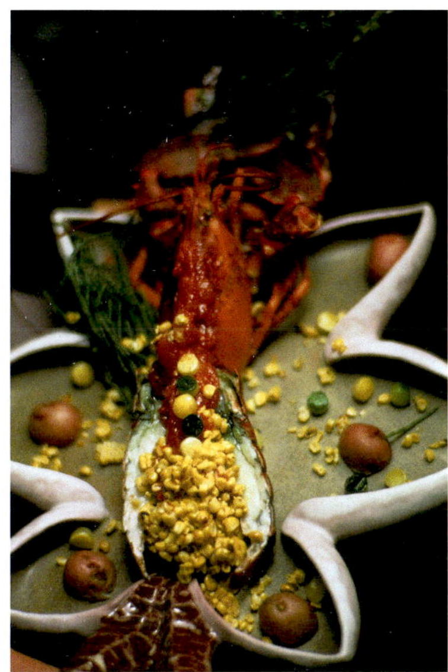

worked with Andy Warhol and had his own theater company, Squat Theater, and he had the most incredible head. I went over to him one day and said, "Peter, I'm going to brashly ask you: I'm an artist. I have this film I'm interested in doing. You would be my ideal Devil character. Would you be interested in playing the part?" He said, "Oh, no, no, no. I'm so sorry. I'm too busy." I said, "I'm so sorry to hear that. You would be perfect." I went back to my table and he came over five minutes later to say, "Tell me more about your project," and it all unfolded from there.

NBA What else were you making and curious about in the mid- to late 1990s, when you were still in New York?

KD I was involved in making a series of vessels of various kinds that extended different landscapes and questions of staging.

NBA Some of the vessels were the *Lady J*s.

KD Yes. I would say all the vessels I've made simultaneously reference body, plant, food or ingestion, and containment. My work became more and more reductive in this period, and interestingly, the more reductive, the more provocative it was. Living in New York, you're always looking for a public bathroom, right? I started imagining a useful tool for this urban predicament, and so I began making the *Lady J*s, thinking I had invented the concept. I was teaching at Hunter College at the time and one of my graduate students brought in a paper version that he had gotten on a flight to India called "Le Funelle," after he had seen one of my porcelain models in an exhibition, and I thought, "Oh, this is wonderful! I love this." But "Le Funelle" was simply a paper funnel, and I recognized that I could reinvent this form in more interesting ways. I made dozens of versions in porcelain inspired by different things: renaissance fountains, medieval codpieces, tools and various body parts. Then I imagined their performative potential and invited artist friends to photograph them using a *Lady J* in exchange for one of their choosing. The photo documentation of the *Lady J*s in use resulted from a desire to see the connection to the body that these objects suggested, and create a theatrical moment for the viewer to witness.

NBA It's so great. A lot of what you had been making while you were in New York was based on these objects of bodily use. Then,

*Lady J*s and *Photos in Use*, 1997. Porcelain, Polaroids, and enameled aluminum, 18 × 84 × 12 inches.

Photograph courtesy Garth Clark Gallery, Santa Fe.

Jacqueline's Lady J in Use, 1997. Polaroid, 4 × 6 inches.

Photograph by India Dunnington.

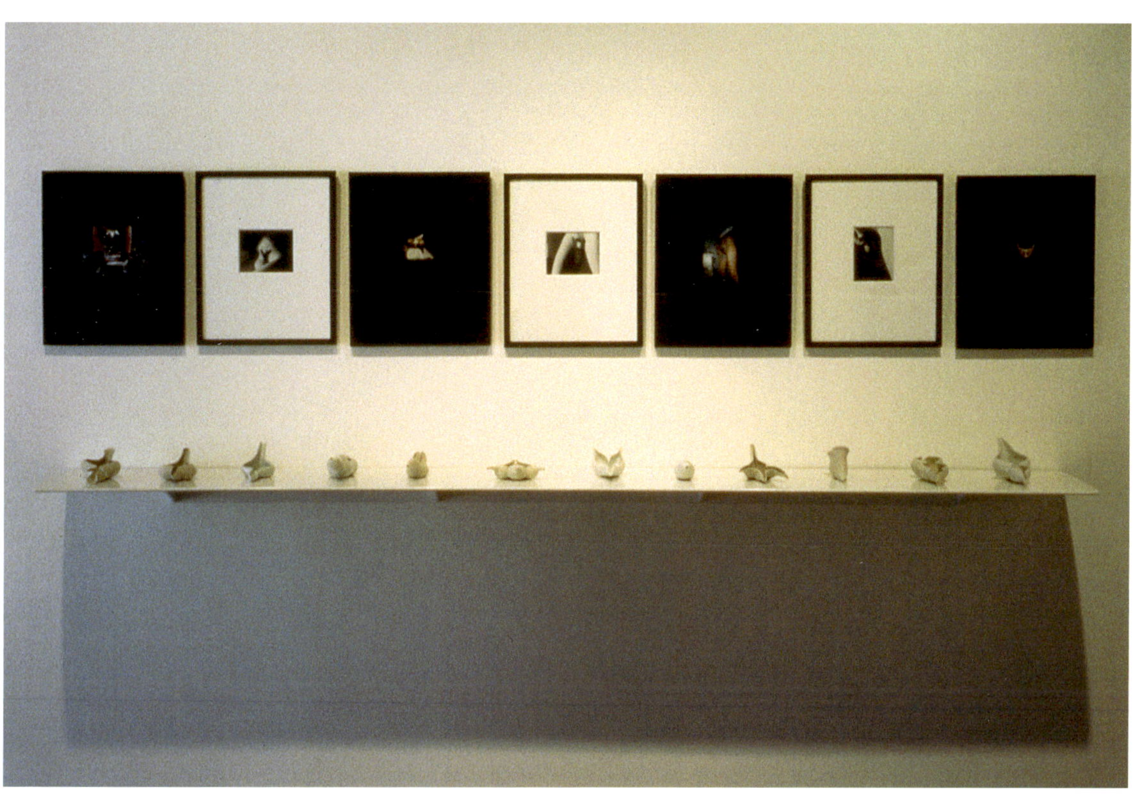

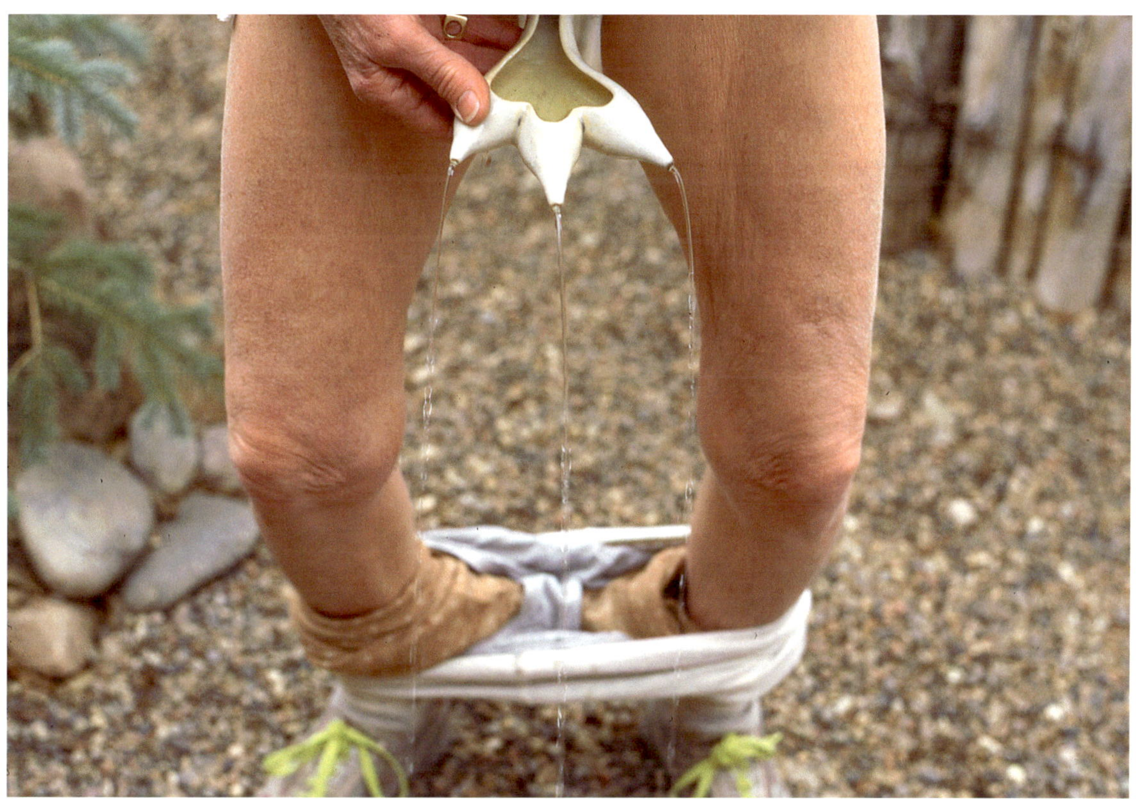

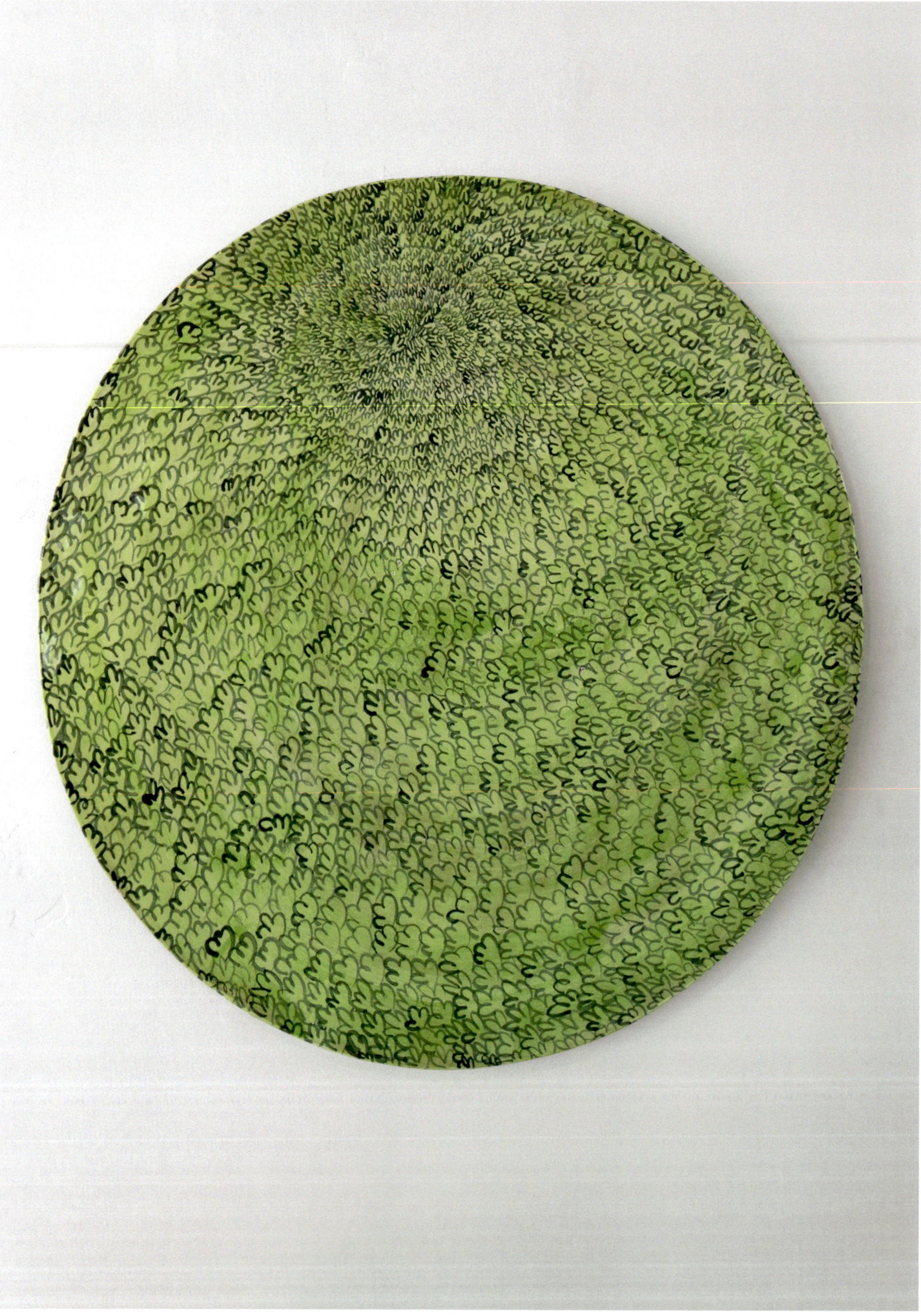

with the performances, you have the body as object. Then you start making—I'm drawing a certain trajectory here, so cut me off if it feels false—but I'm thinking of the prints in which you made plates comprised of body parts. You began in earnest to make ambiguous the body as object and the object as body. And soon after that, the work goes from being able to be handled to something you physically enter.

KD I even think of the garden as an object in the world. It's an enclosed space. It's a container.

NBA There's an inversion of isolated object and environment. What is contained within four walls is as much an object as something that can sit on a pedestal or a table.

KD Or conversely, the table can be seen as a landscape.

NBA That's interesting, that it goes both ways. What was your first manifestation of this?

KD I have always been excited about the potential of an object to promote an entire landscape or to transport us to an entire landscape. In October 2000 Mark Masuoka, then the director of MCA Denver, invited me to be a part of the Colorado Biennial. I gave him this little maquette of an island with a series of palm trees, which I called "Mirage." It was basically an oasis. I said, "I want to make this at real-life scale." That's the first time I created a landscape that one could physically enter.

NBA How did you feel after having created this first actual landscape?

KD It just took off, creating many opportunities and ideas to investigate. For instance, seeing *bocage* in the European museums when I went to teach in Italy in 2000, led me to see objects at different scales and indeed play with scale even further.

NBA What is *bocage*?

KD It's a rococo tradition of intricately sculpted porcelain flowers that are meant to mimic real flowers, specifically botanical representations, that often covered objects like candlesticks and vases, and acted as a backdrop to figure sets and so on. It was borrowed from the theatrical sets of the day and romantic paintings, sort of François Boucher-inspired.

Omphalos, 2015.
Glazed terracotta, 30 × 1 inches.

Photograph courtesy the artist.

NBA It also speaks to ideas about decoration and decorative arts.

KD Absolutely. I've always been interested in lost traditions, things that are overlooked.

NBA Like the *Lady J*s, and also making sculptures of bushes at the size of an actual bush rather than reducing the decoration to being in service of an object.

KD It becomes all surface.

NBA Exactly. You're taking what had been historically used to cover a surface or to make the surface tantalizing, seductive, and making it the focus.

KD The surface is the thing itself.

NBA The surface becomes the object. It speaks to a consistent thread in your practice related to inversion, taking something with strong particular associations and undoing that with a big, grand gesture. Speaking of scale, one important thing to foreground is your critical engagement with minimalism and the monumental sculptures and geometric forms produced in the mid-1960s through the early 1970s, which were intended to reshape how we exist in a particular space. You were well aware of these ideas; I know that they seeded a lot of your thinking.

KD The seeds for all this, you rightly point out, were earlier moments in art history. With my work I've always explored the relation between the private and public, the monumental and the decorative, the realm of language in relationship to objects. Those were all parts of the dialogue in my head. Throughout my life, I've been having conversations with artists of the past. Robert Morris was questioning, "Why can't the plinth be the sculpture? Why can't the architectural form be sculpture?" In turn I'd say, "Yes, why can't it be sculpture—and garden and hedge, and incorporate the decorative?" I'm layering onto his questions questions of my own about what was explicitly or implicitly excluded from the earlier dialogues.

NBA You're intentionally bringing together what seem to be opposing or antithetical traditions. The baroque and minimalism, or the decorative and modernism, or the idea of surface and object, skin and object, something like that. We could probably spend hours enumerating the different binaries. They wrestle with one another in a beautiful way.

KD I hope so.

NBA There are three main groupings that led up to the new installation that we are presenting in the museum: *Cold Pastoral*, *All is Leaf*, and the most recent one, *Claustrum (Cloister).* I think of them as a group, really, each one raising certain ideas and pushing them further. They are remixed in our presentation. Let's talk about the impact of that.

KD In making my last few large installations, I was interested in different psychological experiences that stem from types of landscape or types of architecture. In *Cold Pastoral*, it's the idea of an endless vista created by an *allée*, straight lines and a mirrored back wall, so you become implicated in this endless distance within the gallery.

NBA You see yourself in it.

KD Yet there are side vistas, if you will, formed by the photographic documentation of French formal gardens, that reinforce this expansive view. Then *All is Leaf* also employed a long, narrow space, although I realized that I could do the exact opposite, meaning, create a kind of deconstructed, fragmented garden that had fallen to ruins.

NBA It's also the idea of architecture enclosing or defining the garden as a site, and then things are contained within that. You've taken all of the attributes of a lush garden landscape and embodied them in the objects. Instead of creating a landscape with objects in it, you've created the objects of landscape.

KD They become green walls. They look as though they're alive, sprouting and dying in their variegated surfaces. Inversely, the figures that become statues are also completely foliated.

NBA What are some of those statues?

KD There's the work called *The Departure*, which is a rabbit, completely encased in leaves, leaping into space from the top of a pedestal. It has a frozen quality both in terms of being stone-like, and maybe even turned to stone, and being white. Yet it's also being subsumed by leaves as though it's been encroached upon, overgrown. I think this suggests a somewhat apocalyptic view of another kind of metaphorical "fall." Both high modernism and the baroque period experienced falls from grace.

Then *Claustrum (Cloister)*, which is the latest one, engaged the idea of truly interior spaces that mirror the space of the mind. The architectural sites that I'm referencing here are real sites that are spaces of repose for what was a very prescribed life for monks. They lived within strict confines, both moral and physical. The cloister garden was a place where they could speak, eat, read, share stories. The sculptures in this installation served as interior voices meant to caution, and also to embody the character flaws and strengths of the inhabitants.

NBA One thing that we haven't talked about yet is the title of the exhibition, *Words Are Leaves*.

KD It's borrowed from a George Ohr placard. He was a Biloxi, Mississippi–based potter working at the turn of the last century. I've read many of his short writings, his placards, and felt a strong affinity to the metaphoric binding that Ohr enacted between language and landscape. One of my favorites begins, "Words are leaves. Deeds are fruit." It's an ambiguous statement, but I wondered if Ohr was suggesting that speech is meaningless, actions are everything. I wanted to question that premise, and by separating the phrases conversely suggest that words, while they're ubiquitous and litter the landscape like leaves, can sustain life. Words may seem cheap if you have been given a voice in this world, but be of great value and privilege if you haven't. So yes, words are leaves and they're deeply, richly potent and elemental to our existence.

NBA Let's briefly turn to some of the new work, such as the series inspired by the rabbit hunt tapestry.

KD It's part of an ongoing fascination with such tapestries. Mirages, illusions—the illusion of a pierced picture plane is so fabulous. There's so much action going on and so much hidden. I'm always interested in the thing you're not supposed to be looking at, the thing that's outside of the action—the backdrop. When I came upon the rabbit hunts at the Burrell Collection in Glasgow, I found the rabbits so funny because they're appearing

Peasants preparing to hunt rabbits with ferrets (detail), Flemish, 1450–75. Wool and silk tapestry, 127 3/16 × 118 1/8 inches.

Burrell Collection, Glasgow.

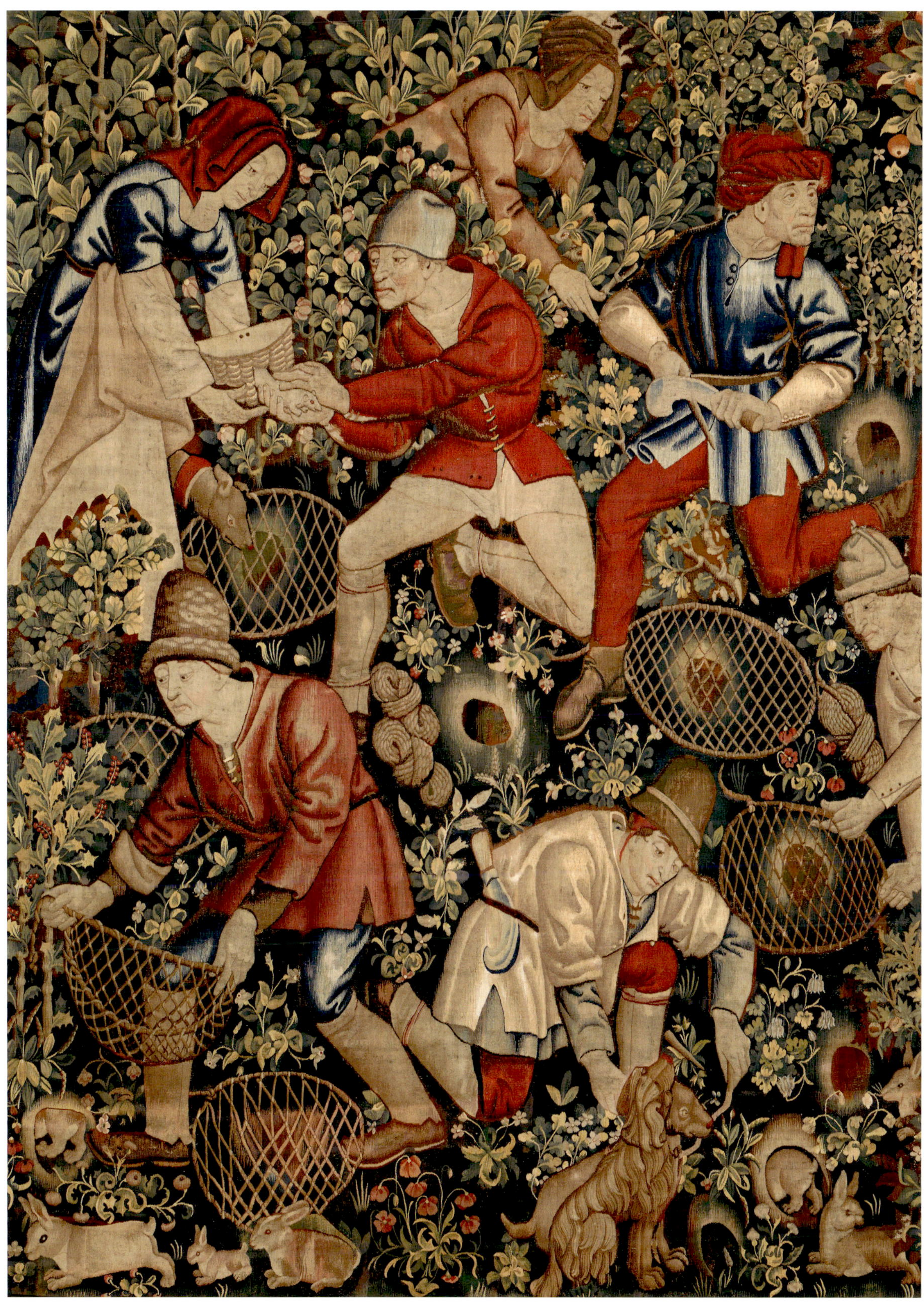

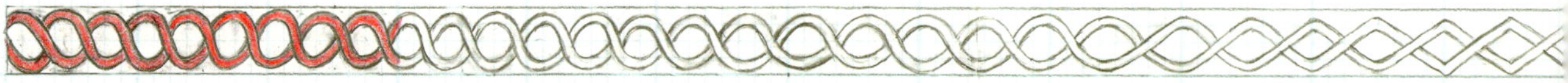

Proposal #2 For Rota do Românico do Vale do Sousa, PORTUGAL

Tile Line installed in outside wall of Pombeiro arcade

"Knots"

Kim Dickey   October 2007

and disappearing. And there's netting and dogs, pointing women and lunging men, all engaged in a futile attempt to try to capture the rabbits. And meanwhile all these holes, rabbit warrens, are punctuating the space of the tapestry, and then ultimately the space of the wall. Rabbits are so closely associated with time; and they're constantly eluding us.

NBA Tell me about the wall drawing that is the final enclosure in the exhibition.

KD In 2007 I was invited by Scott Chamberlin, who was working on a project with the Portuguese government, to tour the Romanesque Route. They wanted to link up all their Romanesque churches and commission a number of contemporary art installations on these sites that would develop it into a cultural tour and attraction. I filled a whole notebook with drawings of details from about fifteen churches. What most took hold of my imagination were the many knot patterns around the exteriors of the stone churches—and many of the interiors as well—and how they evolve and change from church to church. I ended up taking these drawings and weaving them together into one continuous web of two lines. I originally proposed a tile project to wrap one wall of a monastery with this ever-evolving knot, expanding and contracting in different ways. I saw it as history, familial history, cultural history, male-female history.

NBA Coming together and then loosening. I think it's so important to produce it in the exhibition because it epitomizes this idea of baroque modernism that characterizes your work. Your wall drawing, in terms of its subject matter, is about bringing things together and letting them spread out and then come back together. But conceptually, this work is also about conjoining these two very different strands, literally, of your work: the attachment to both decorative arts and conceptual art.

I think what is going to be unexpected for a lot of visitors is that this culminating work is not a sculpture—that it's architecturally bound, and it is about architectural binding. It is both describing certain ideas, and embodying or enacting them. Not only does it enclose, but it is also *about* enclosure. Not only does it bring two very disparate traditions together, but it is also *about* bringing together.

Lineage, 2007.
Graphite on paper, 11 × 64½ inches.

KD I agree—it really becomes the punctuation mark of the entire exhibition. Thank you, Nora.

Words Are Leaves

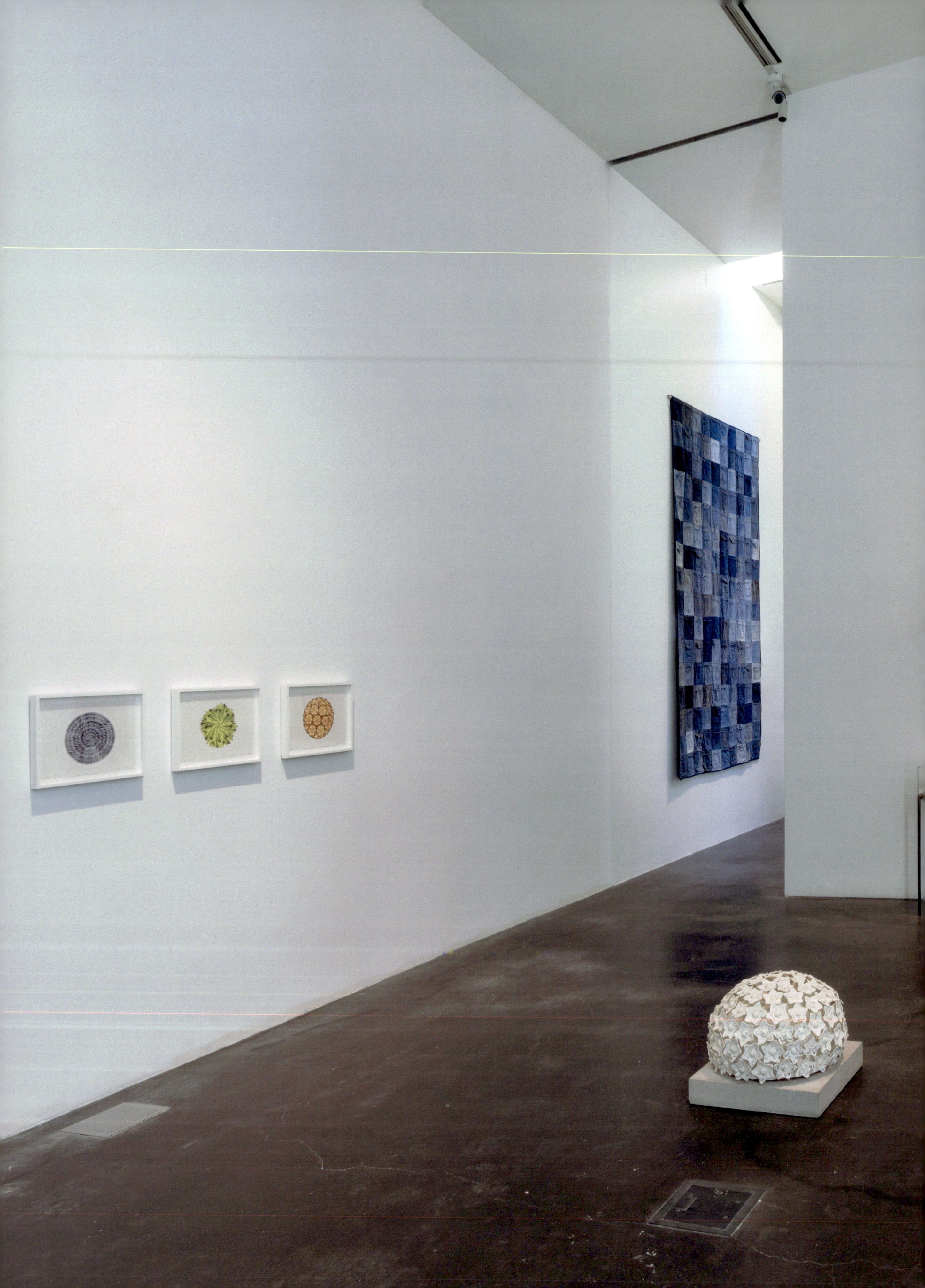

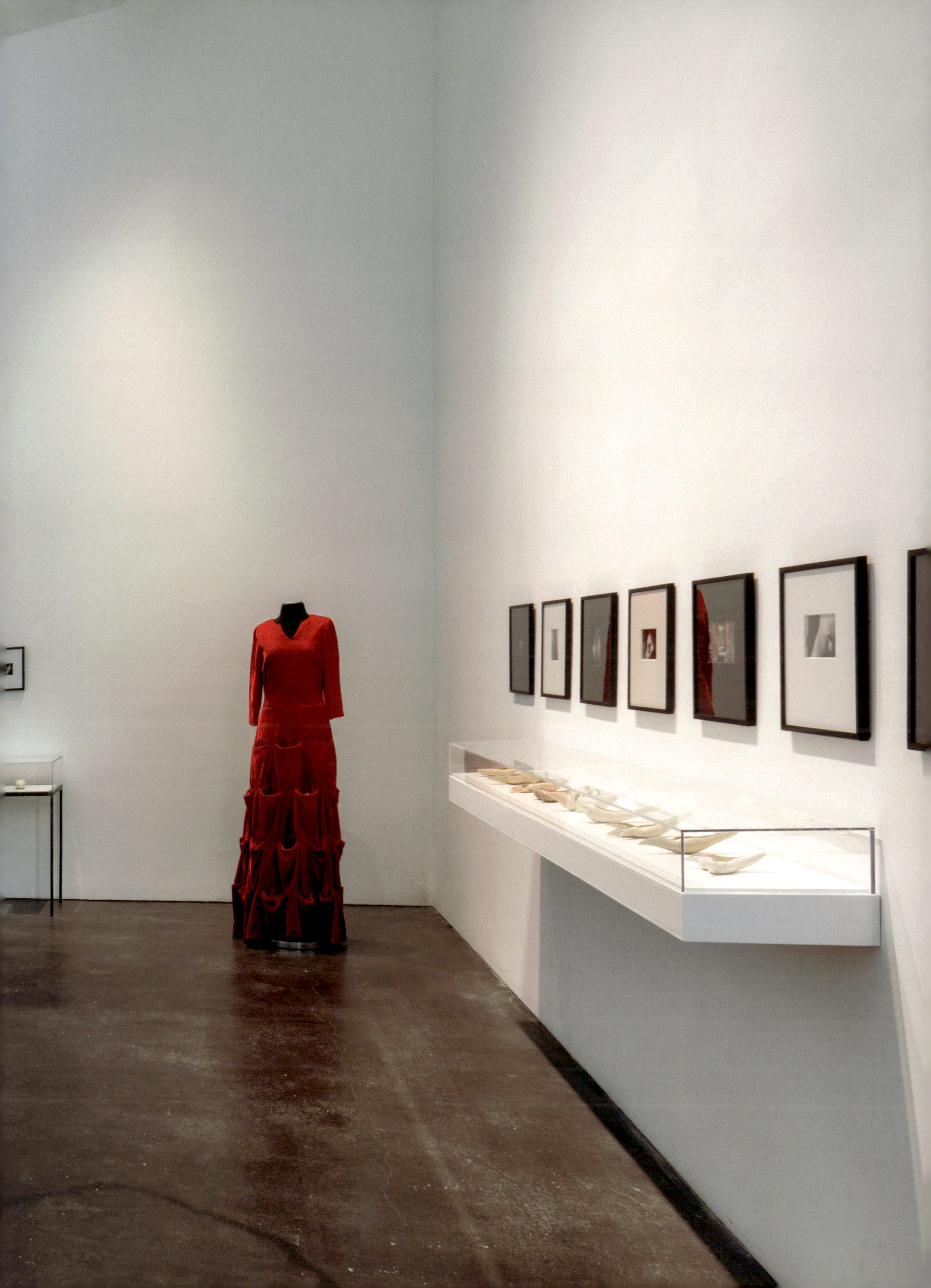

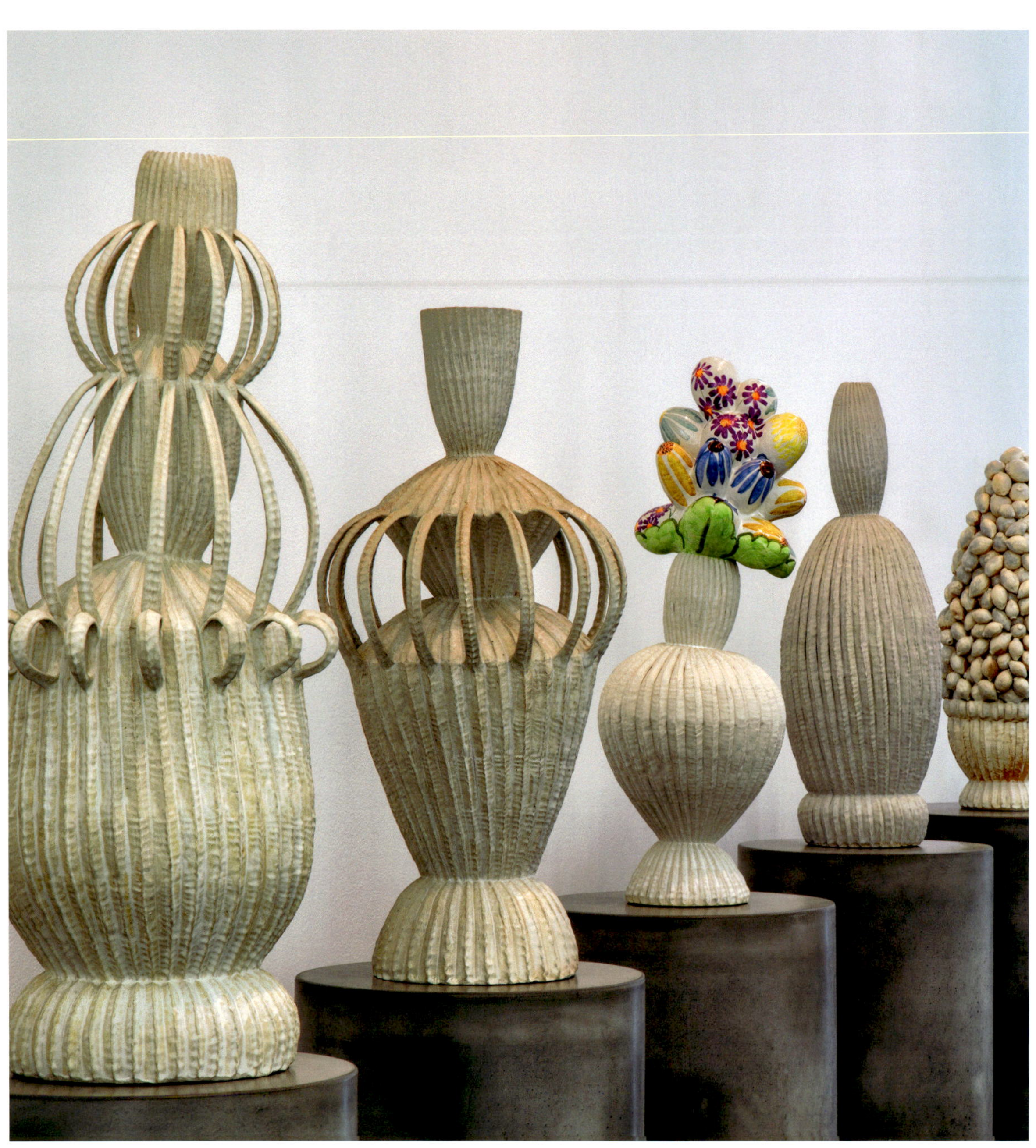

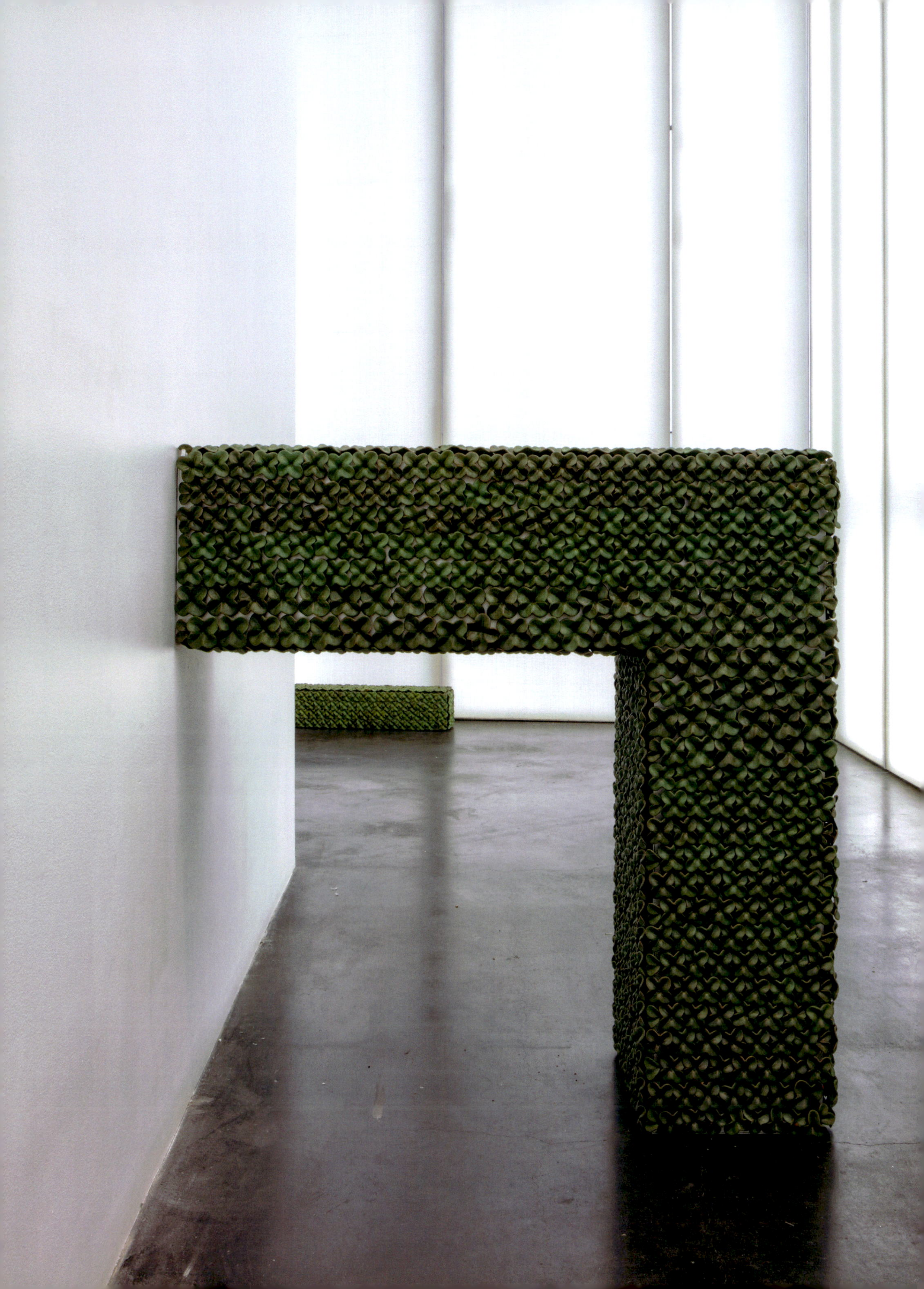

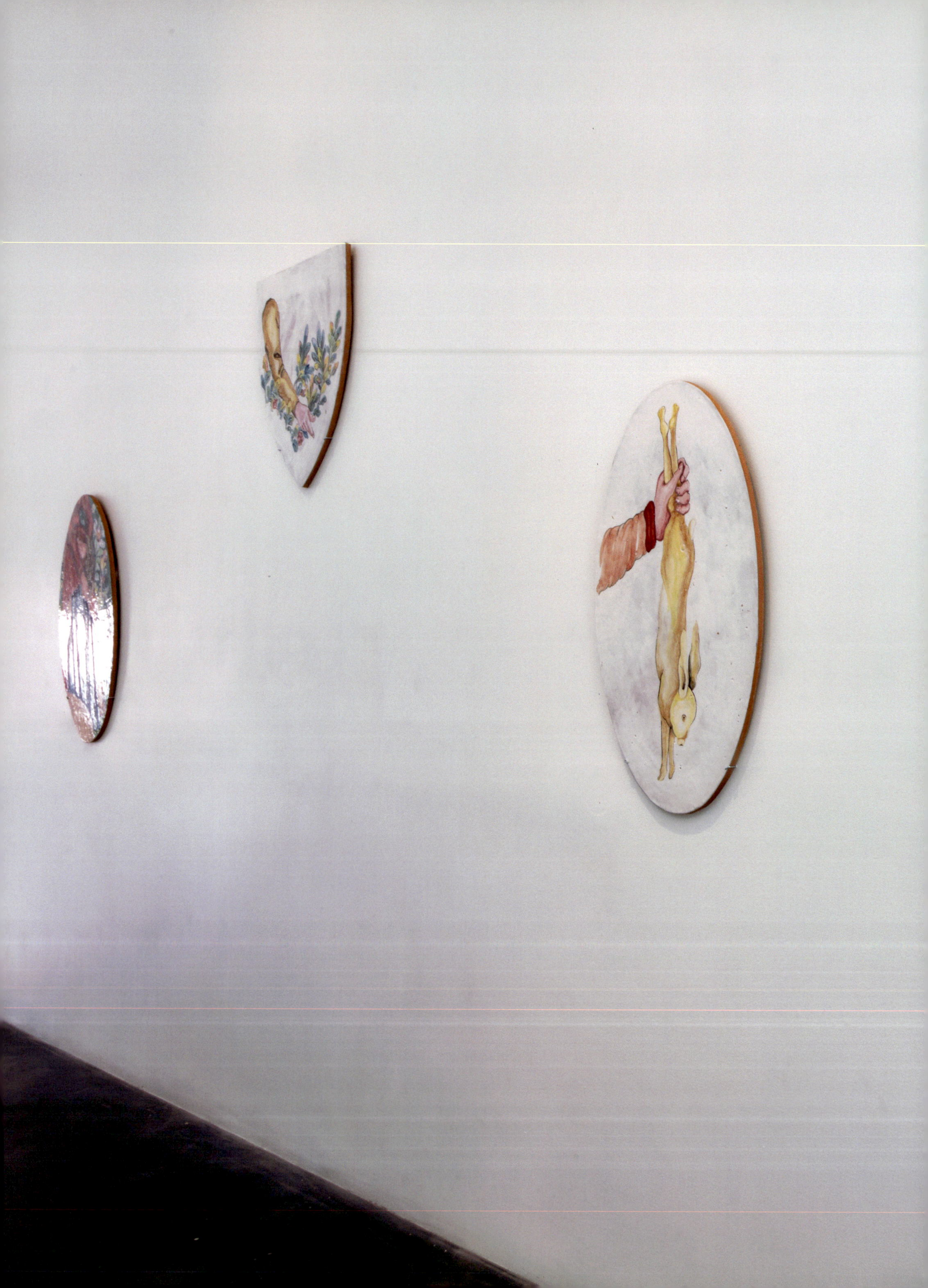

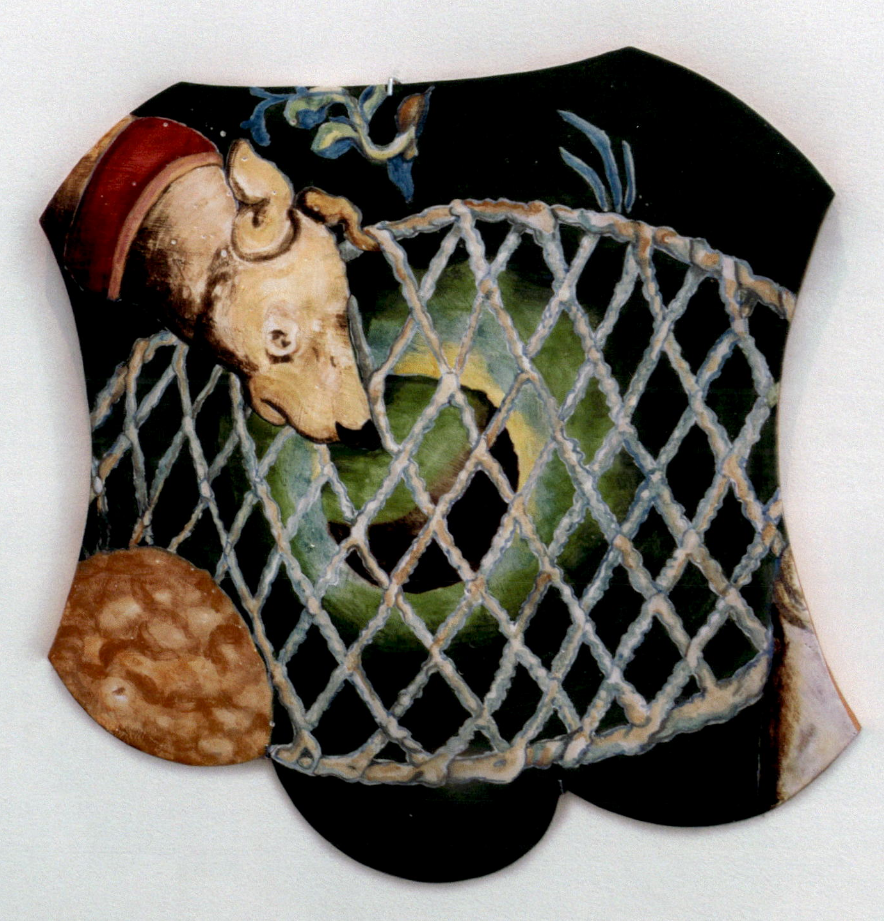

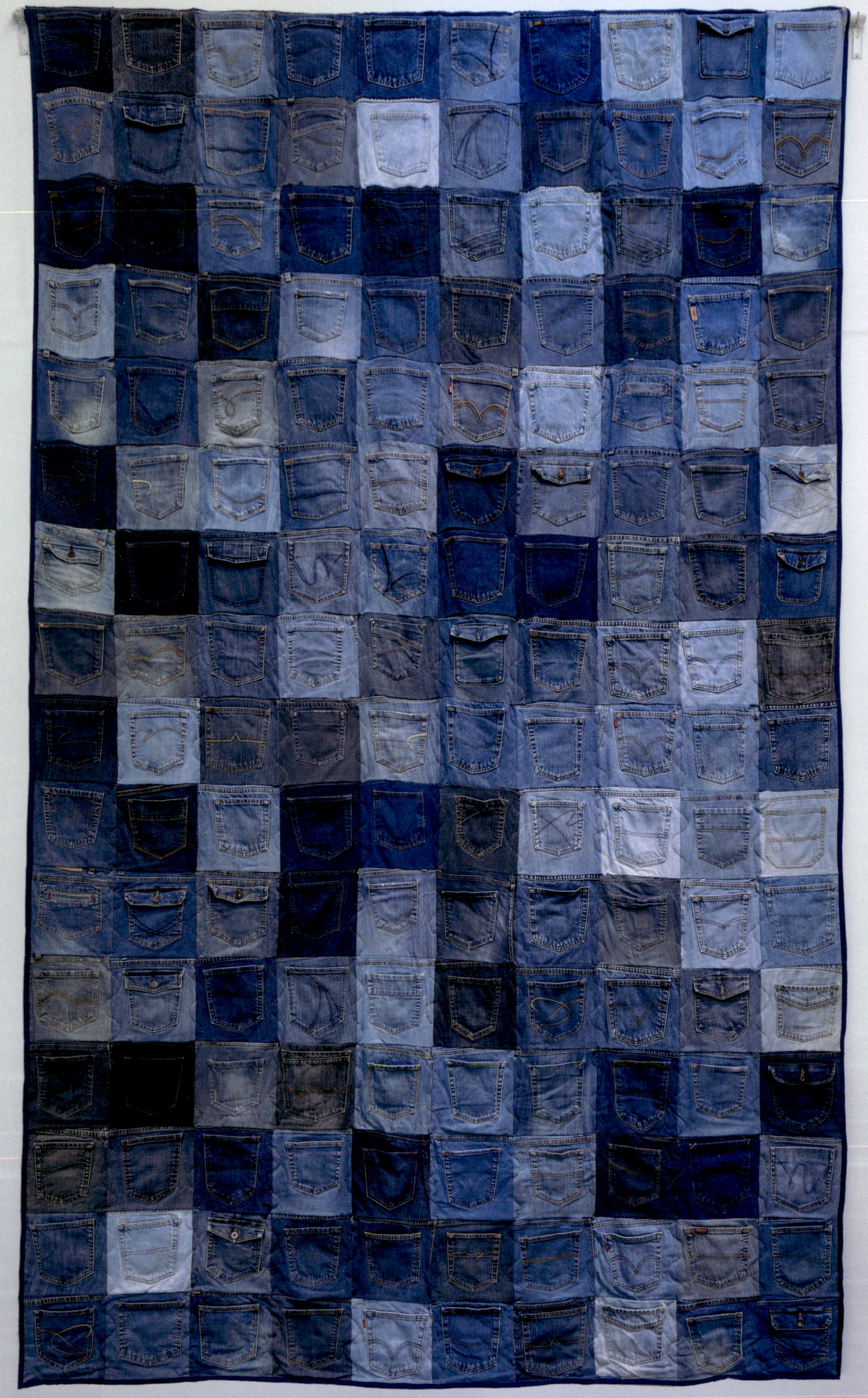

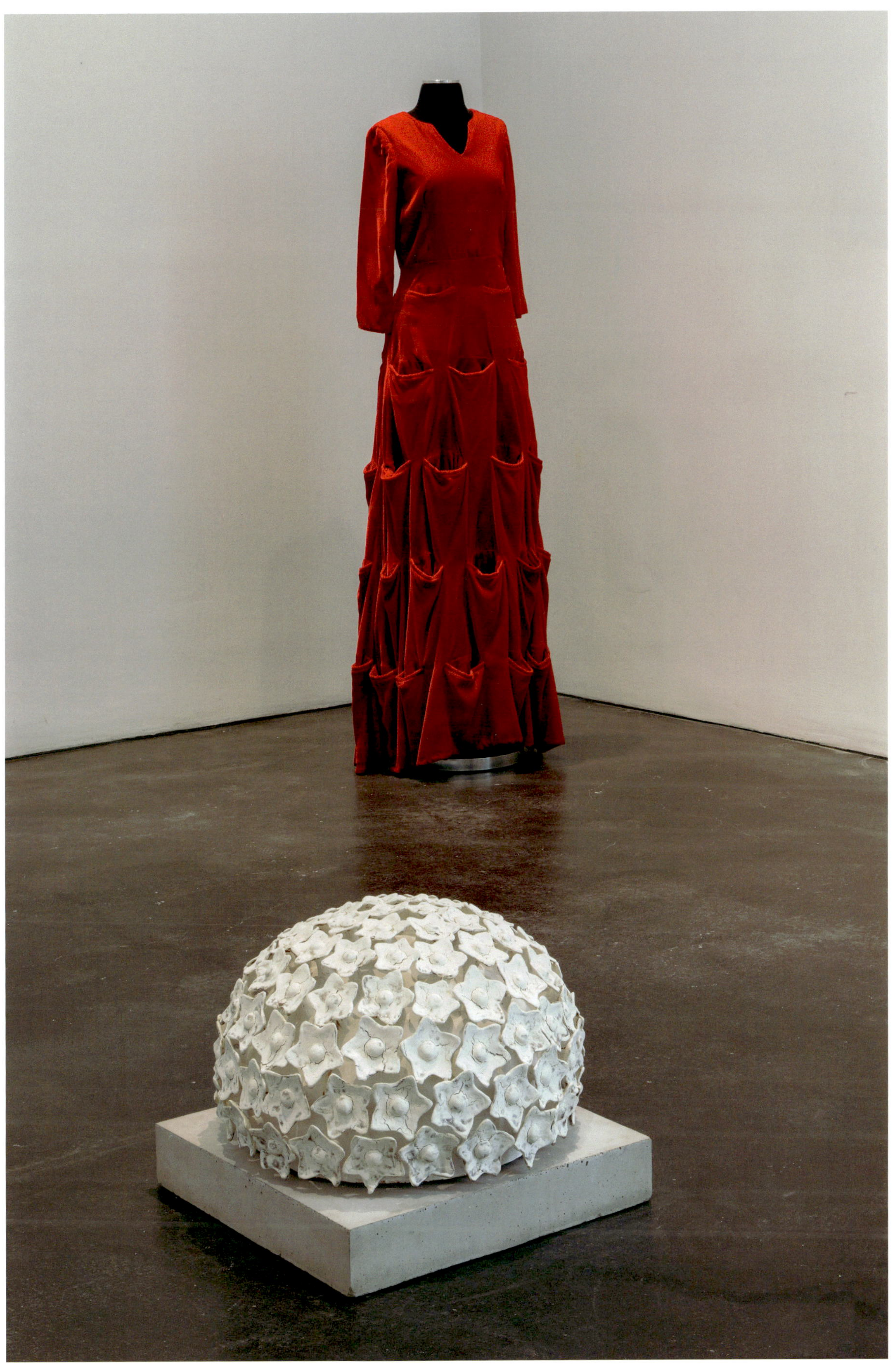

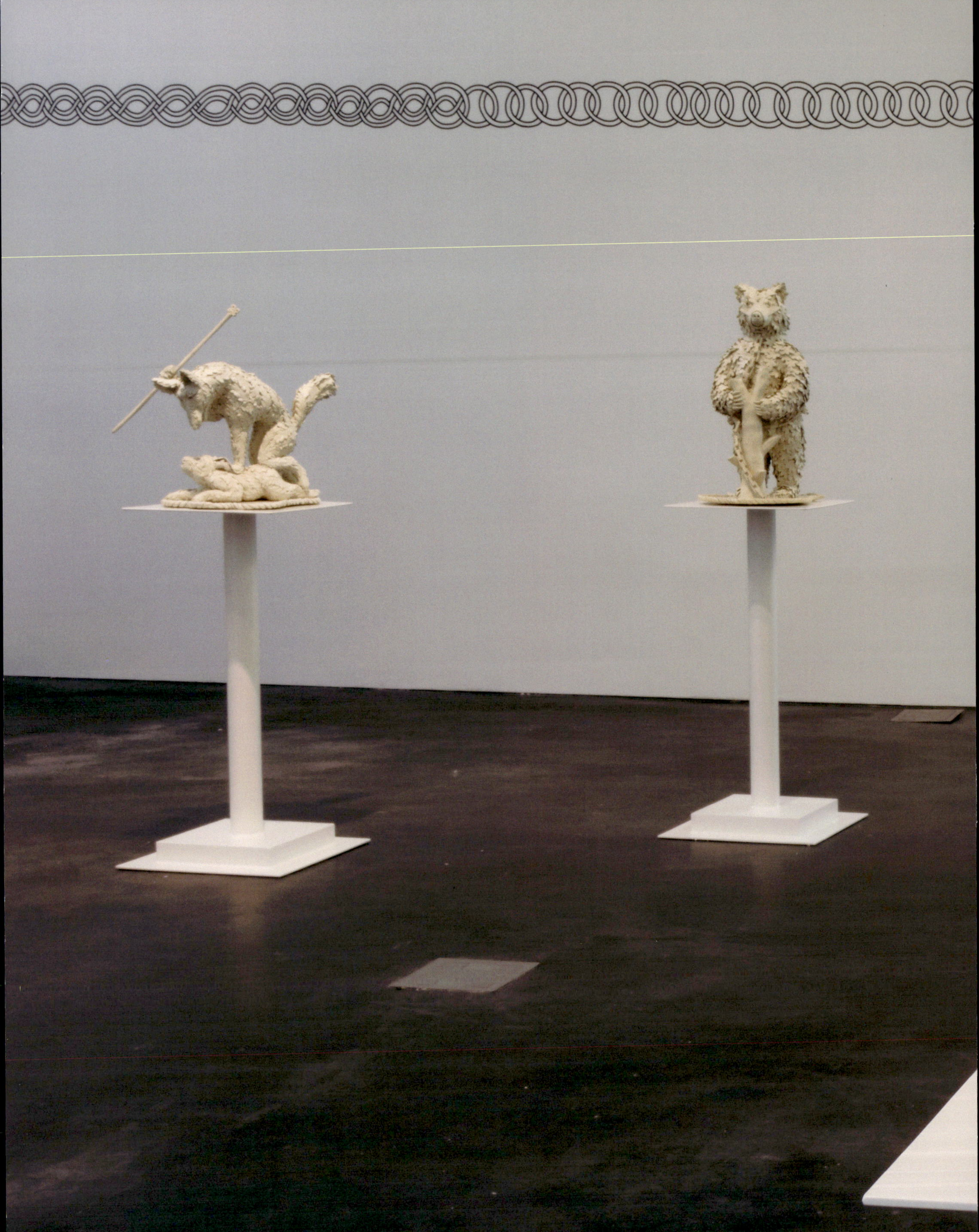

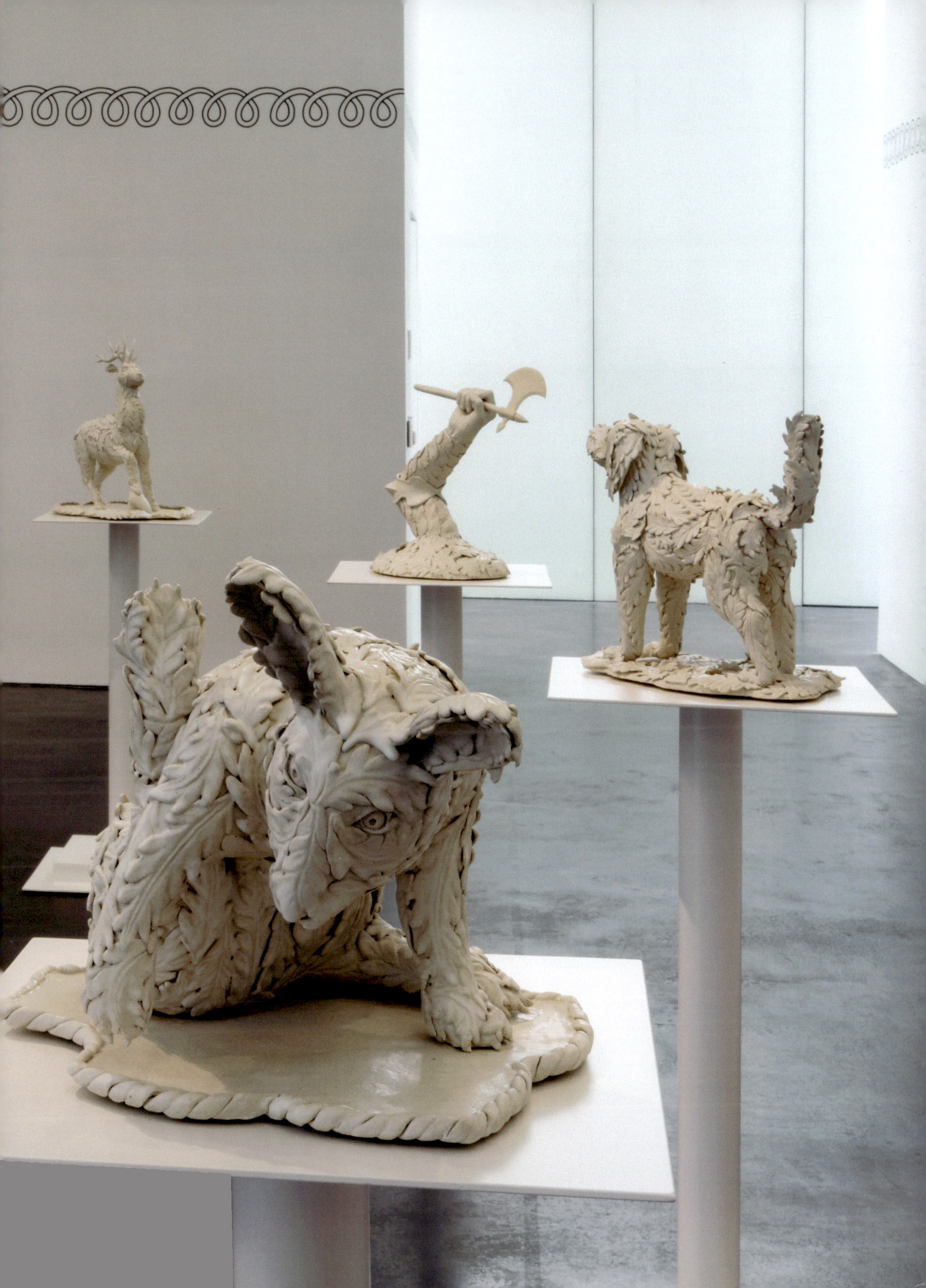

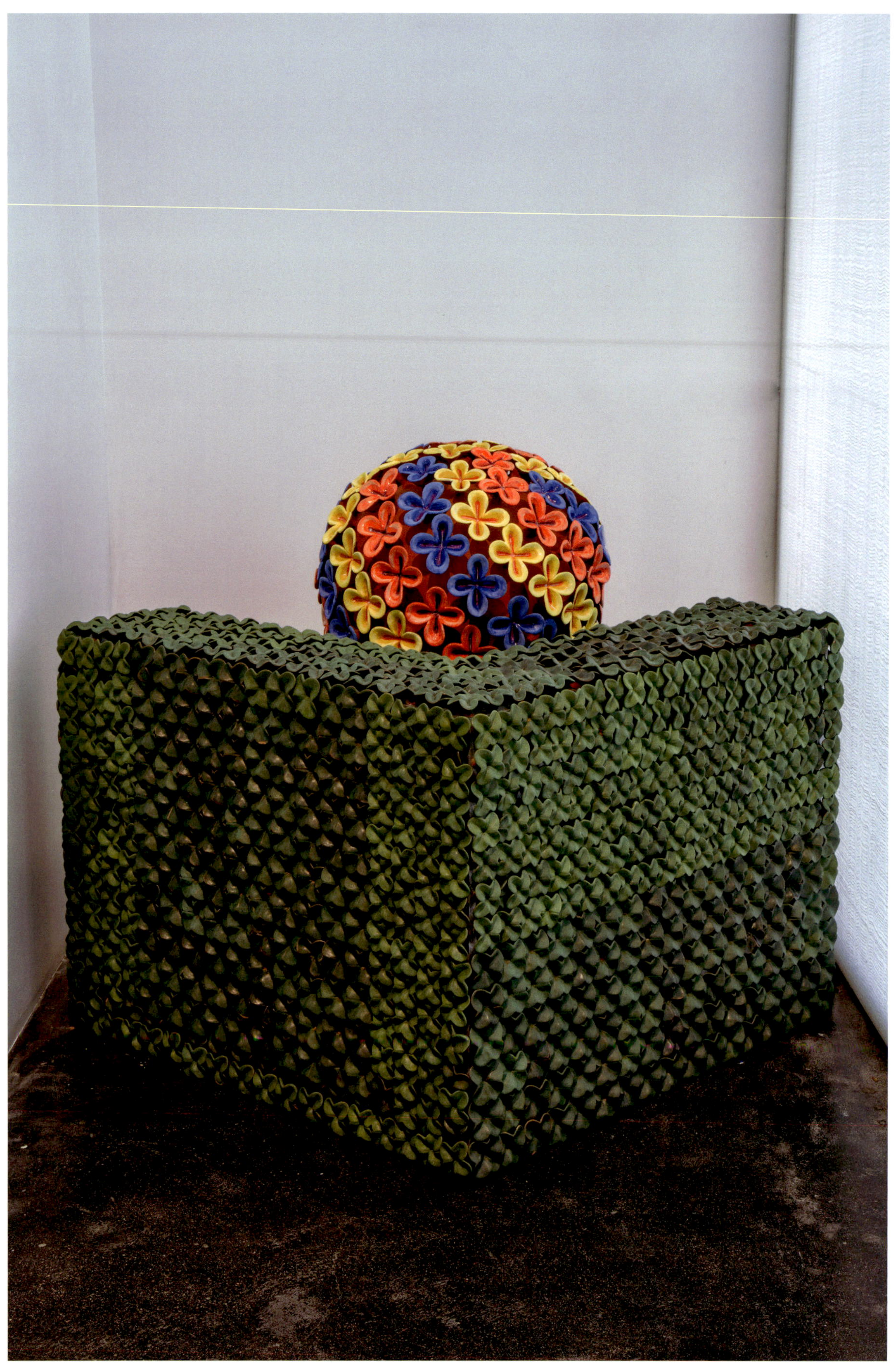

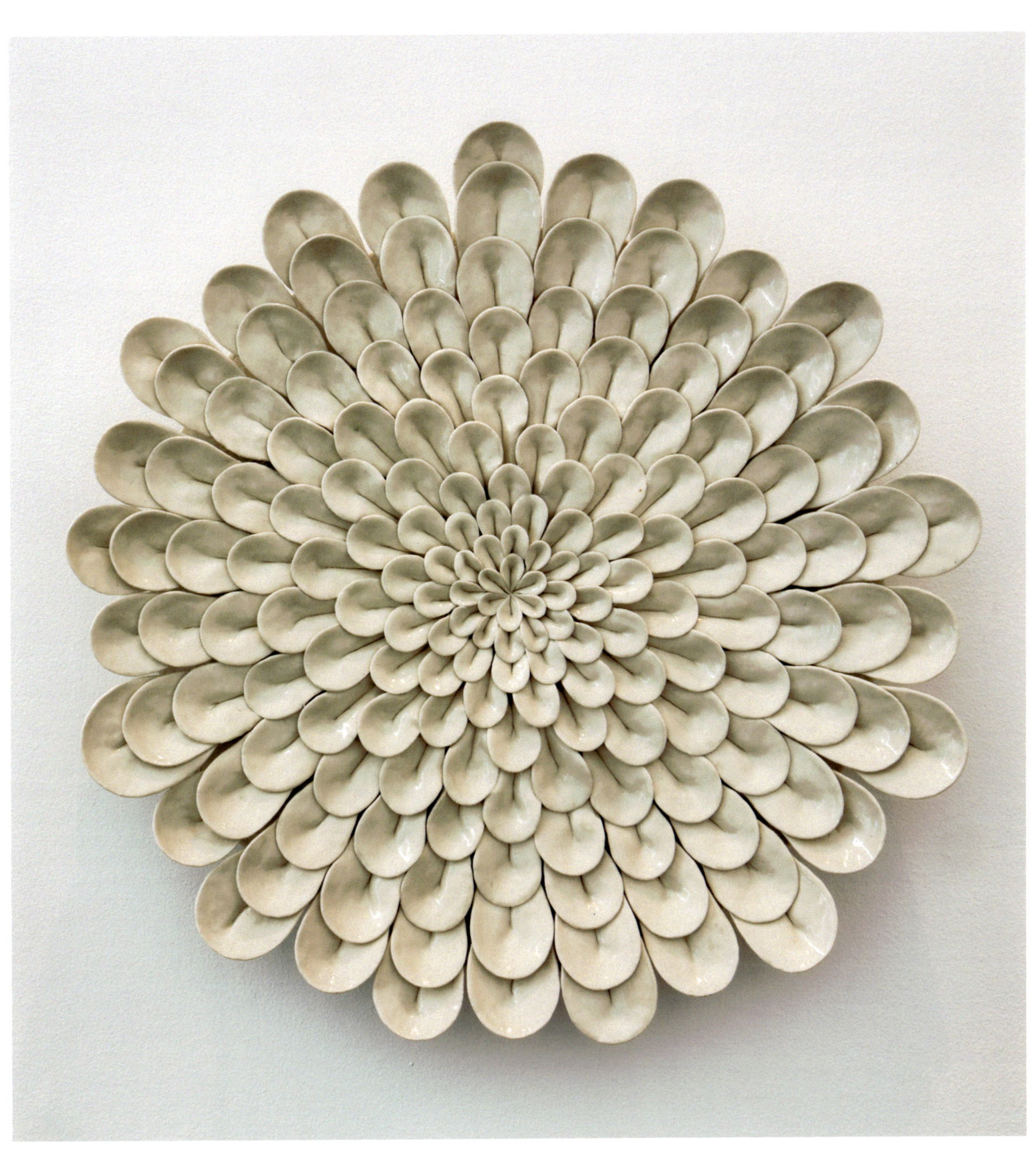

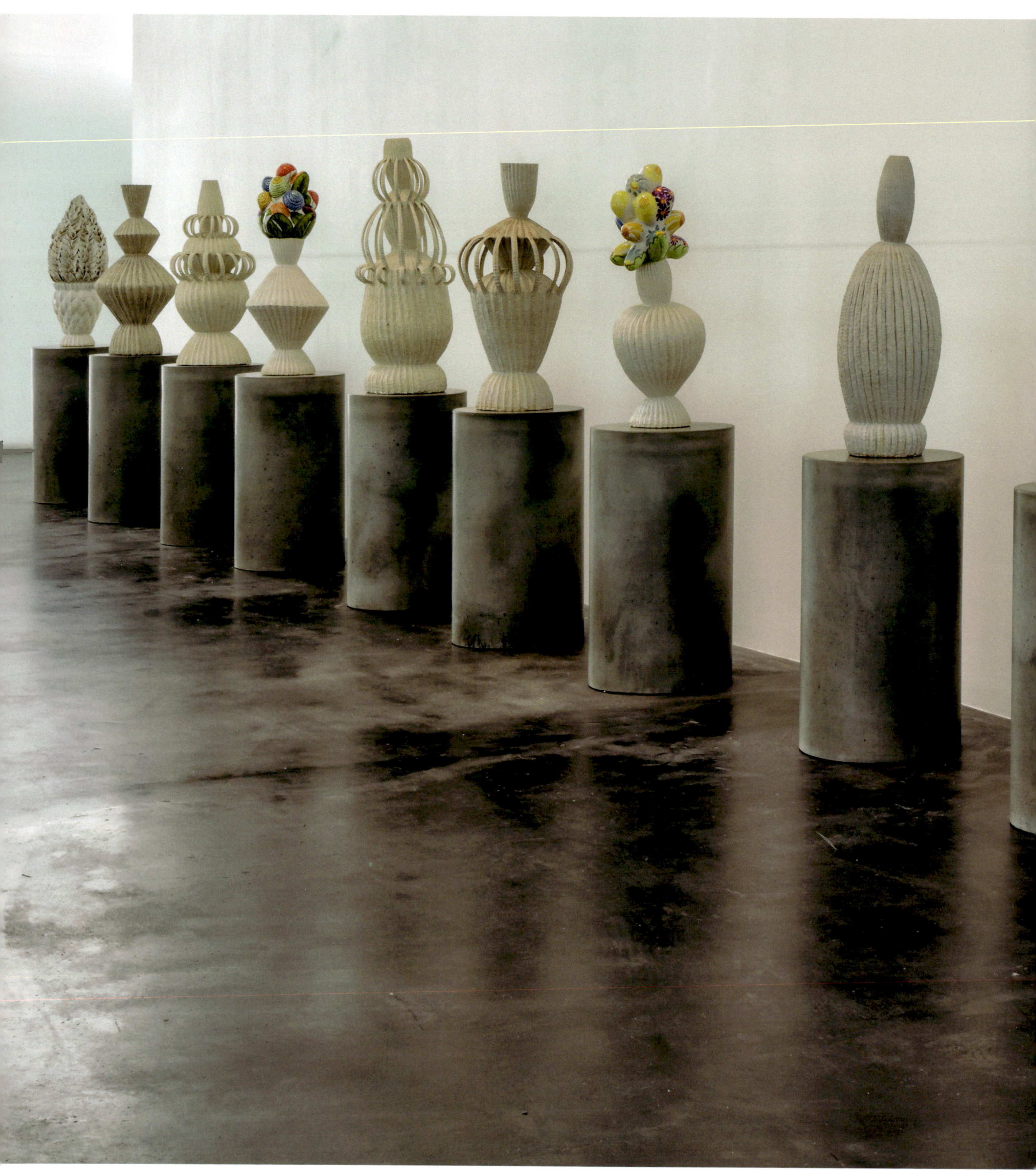

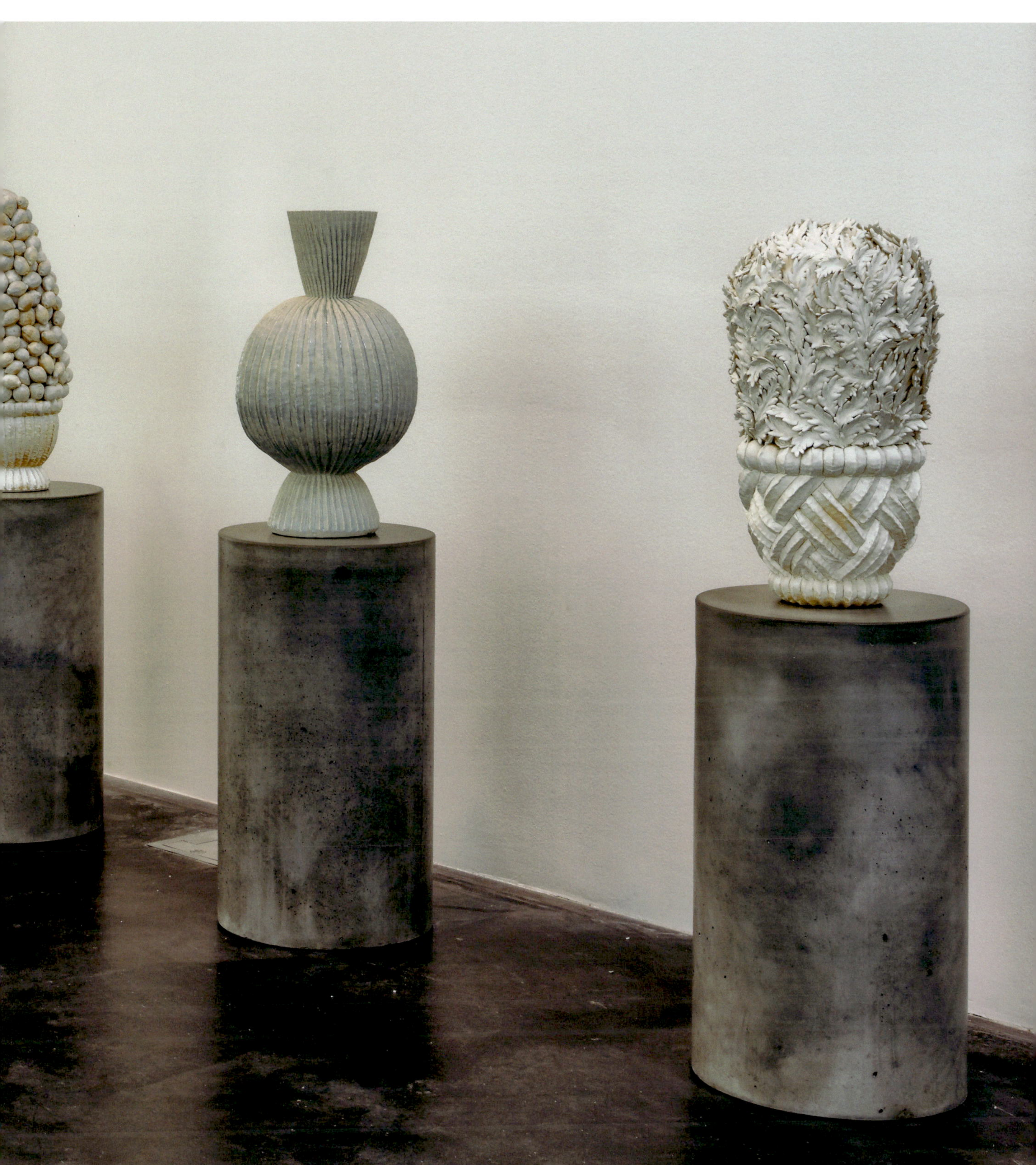

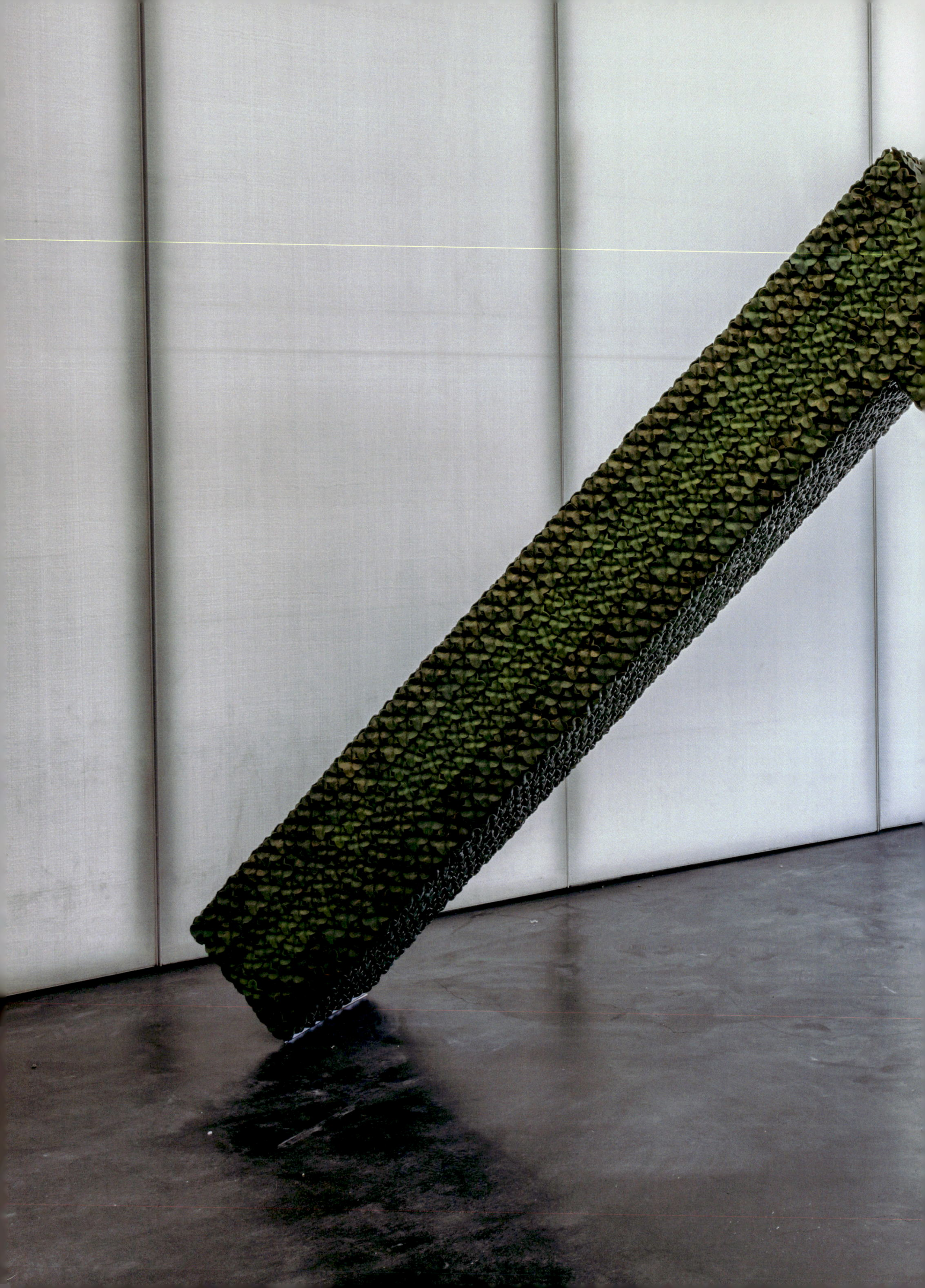

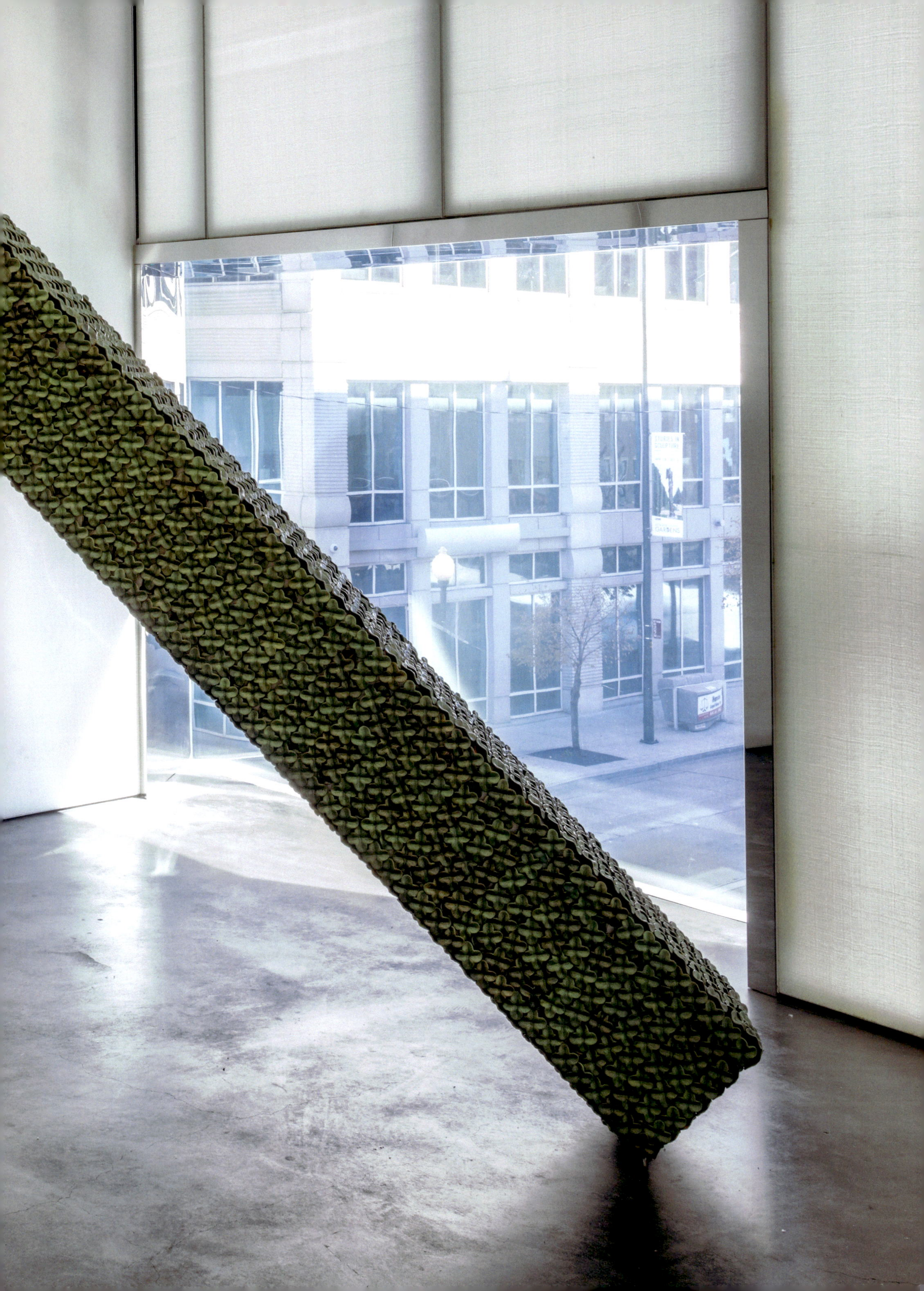

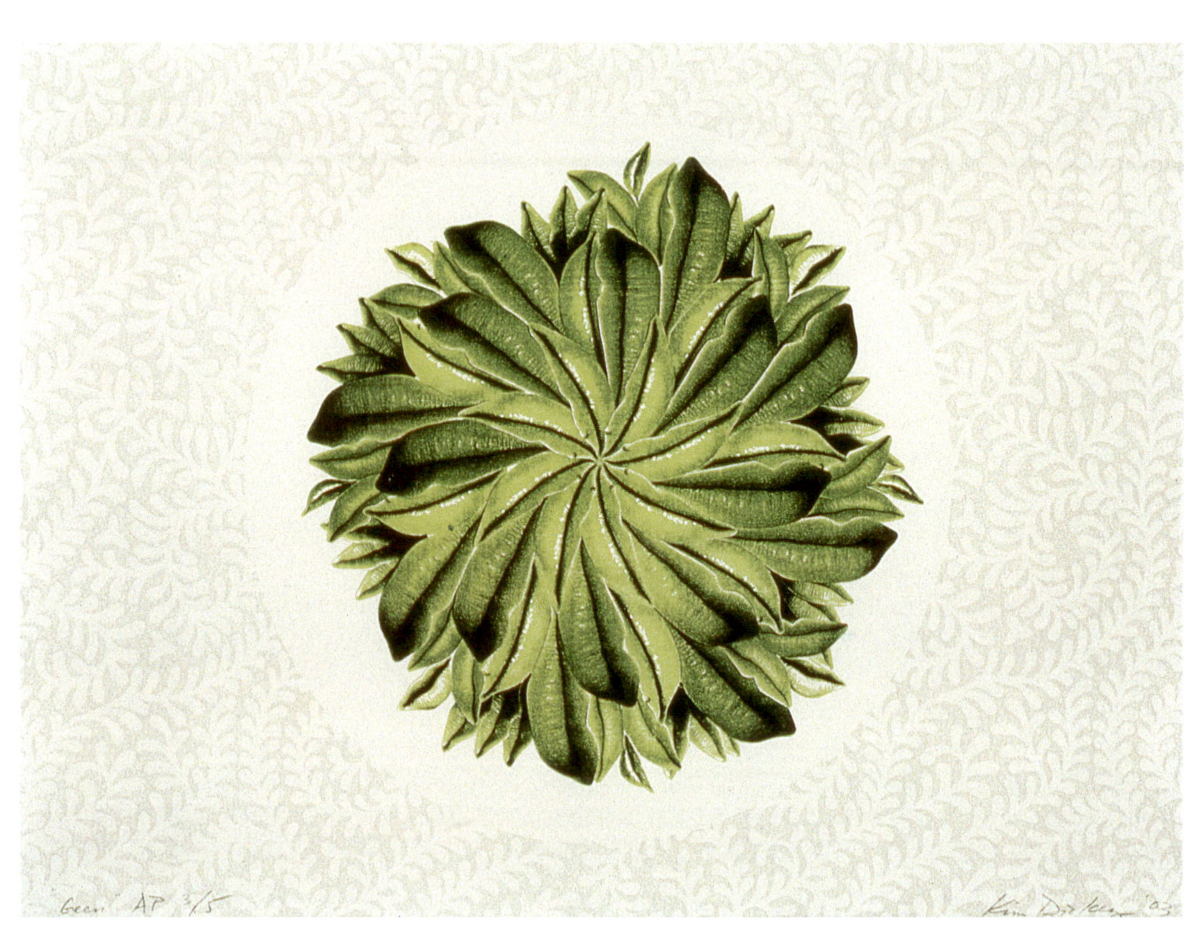

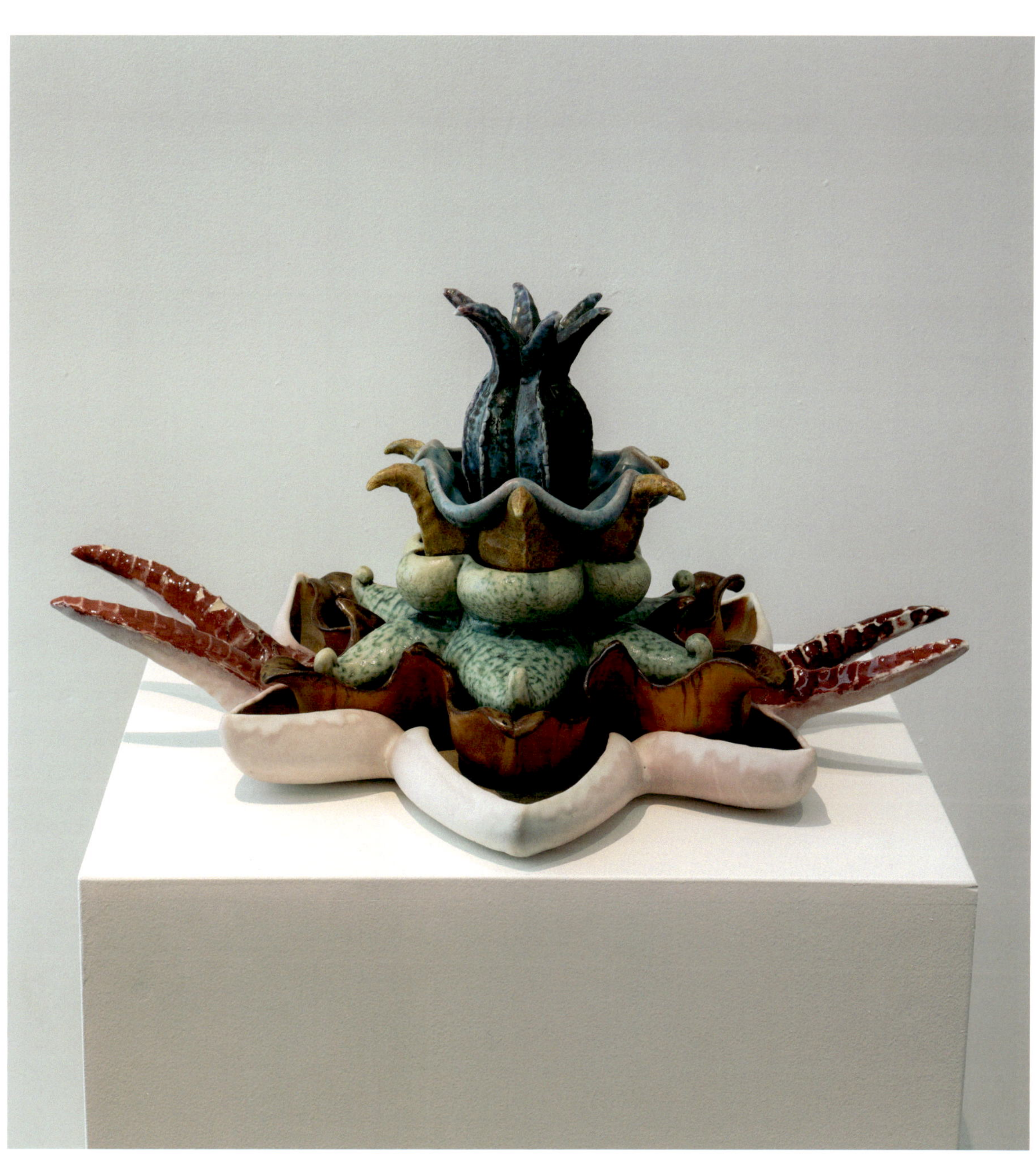

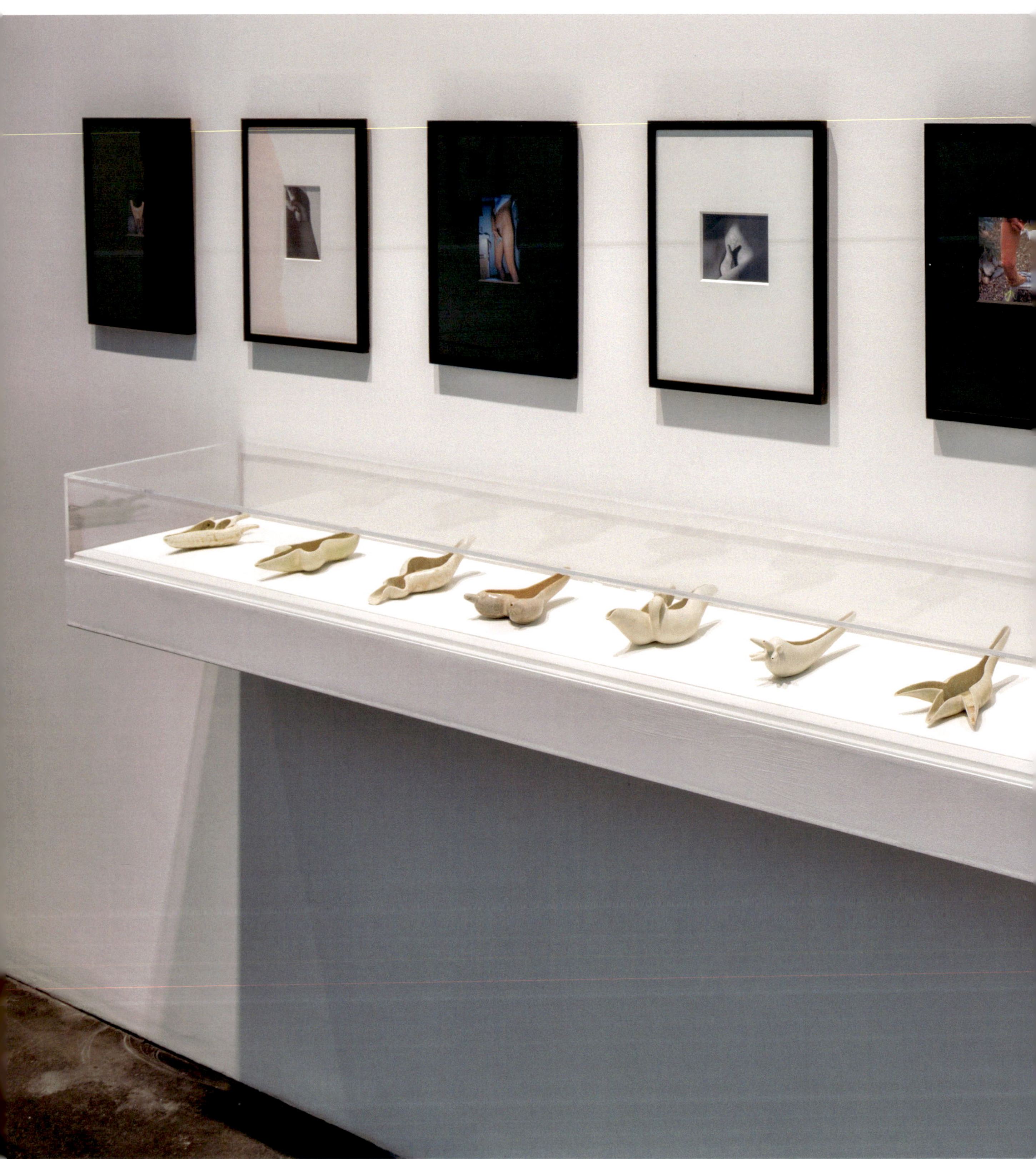

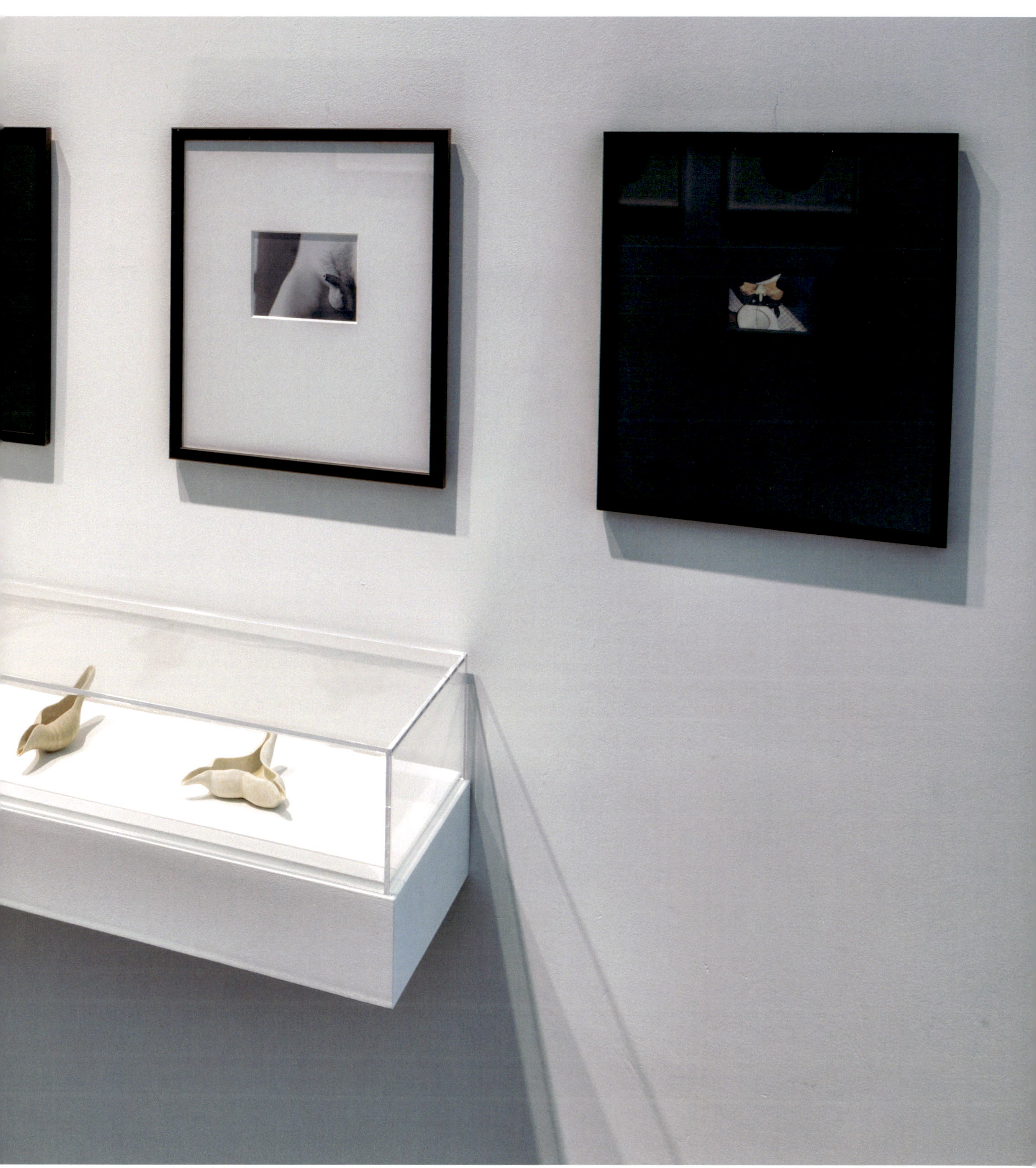

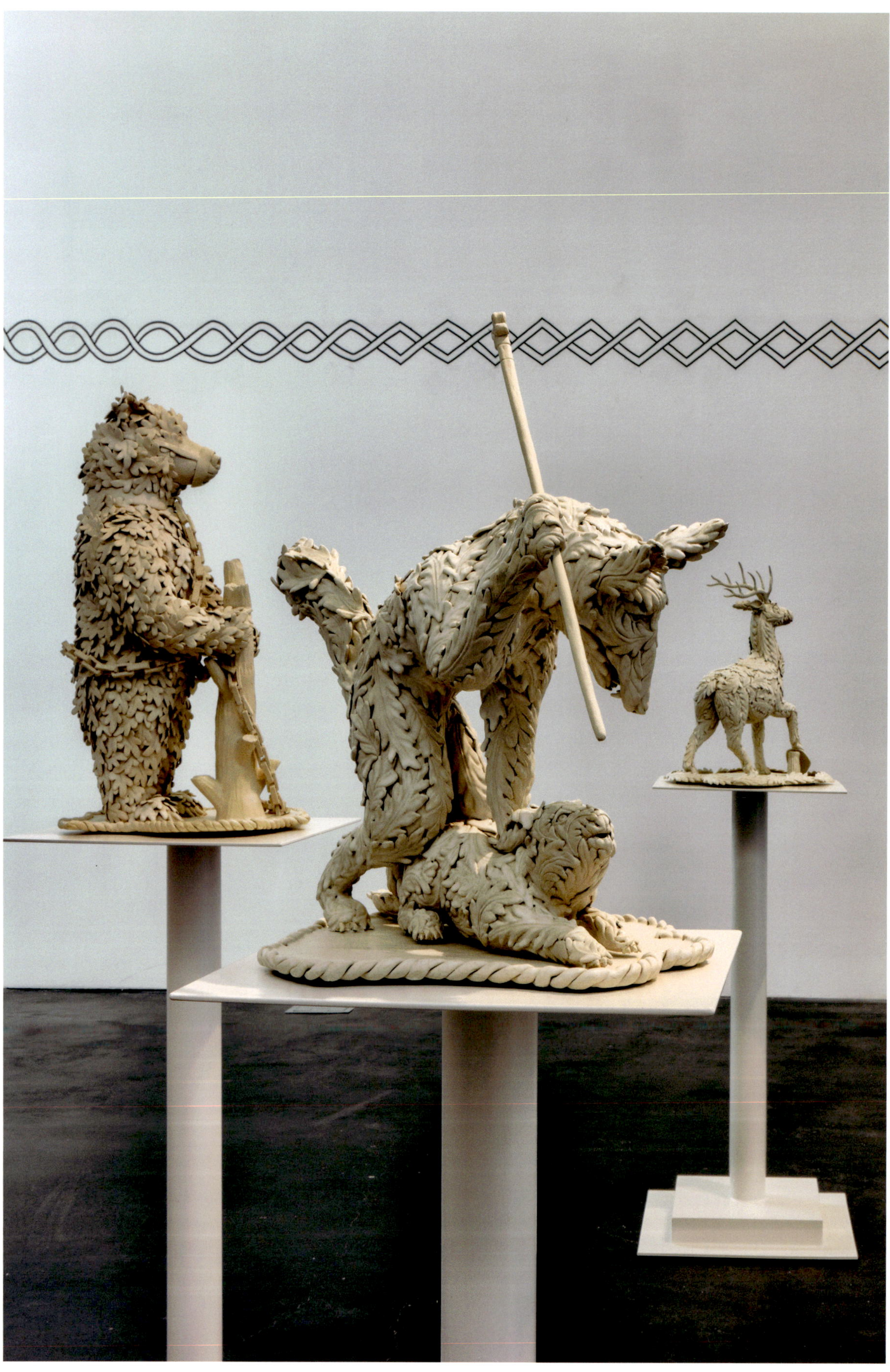

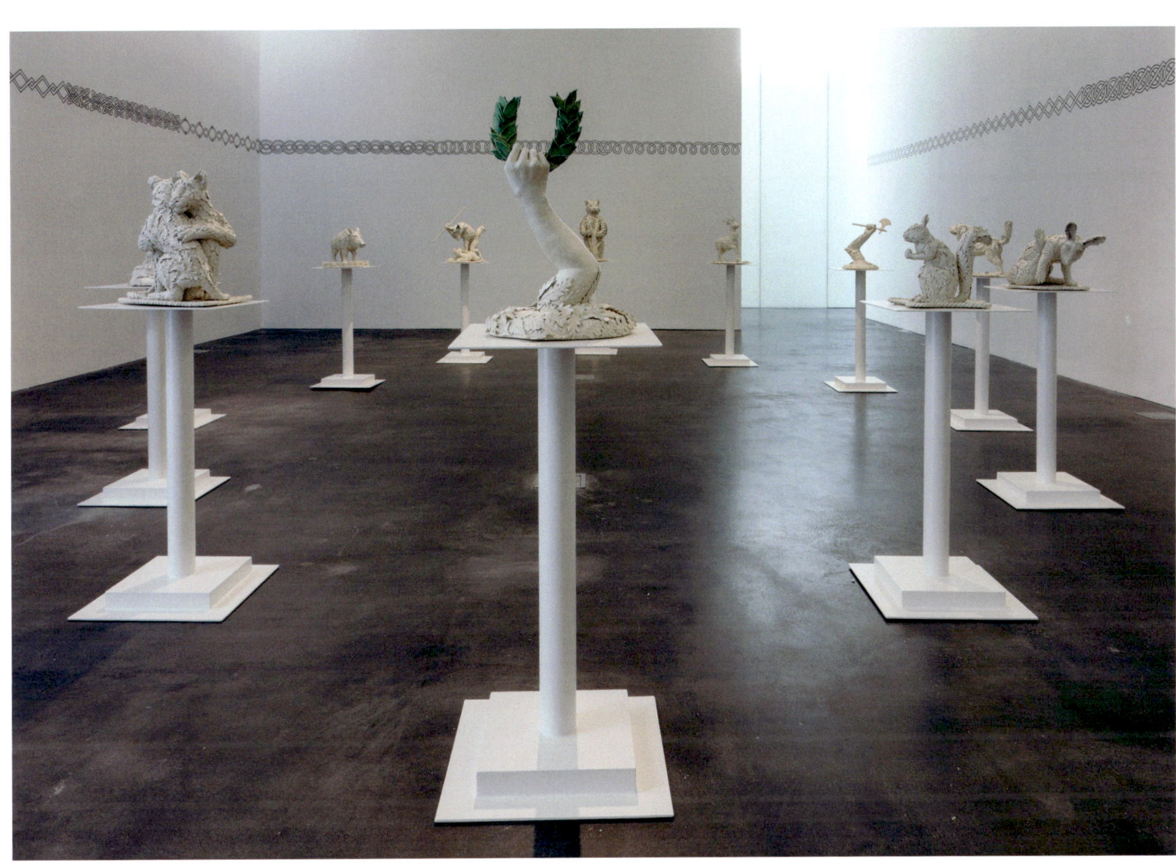

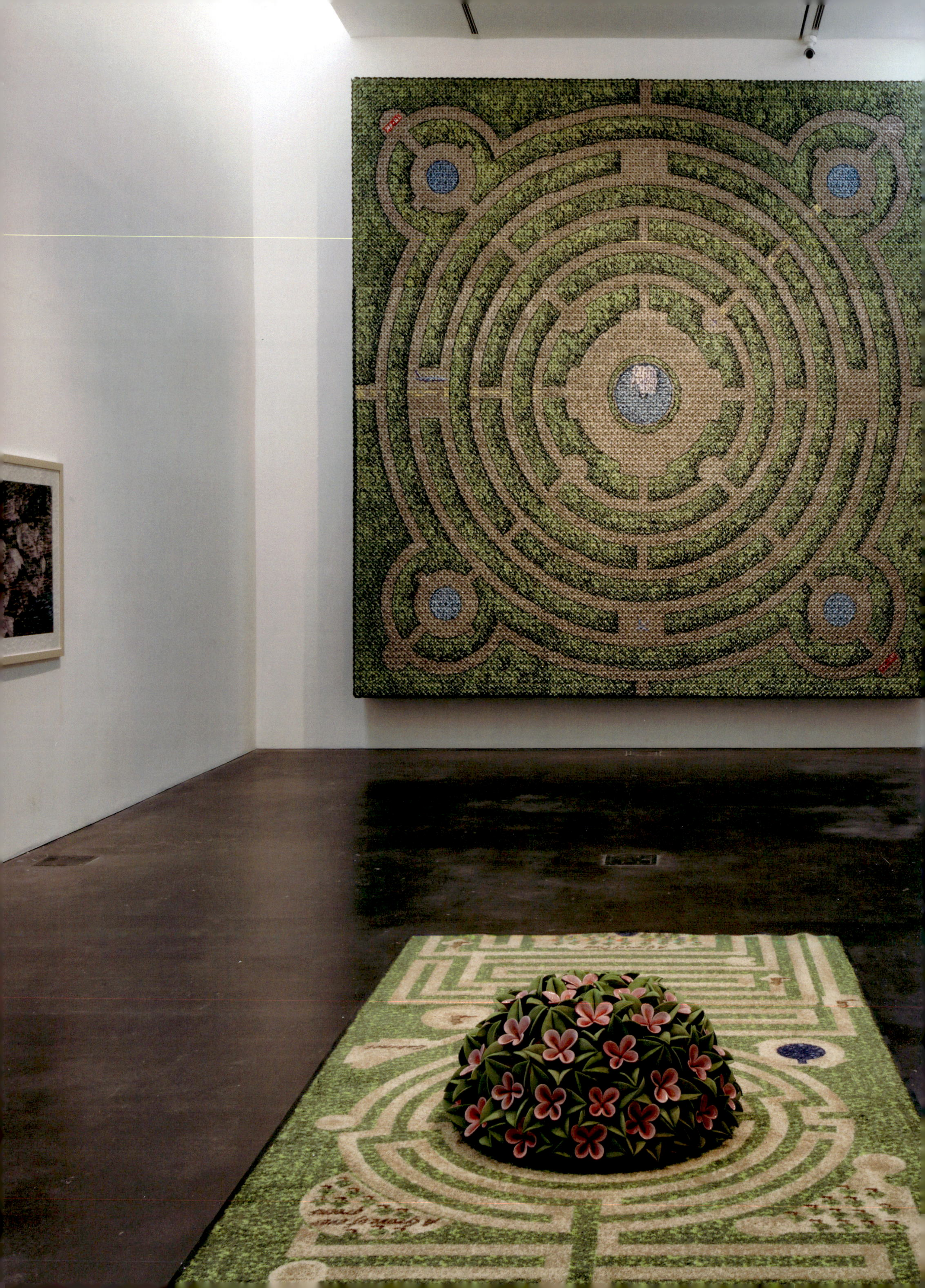

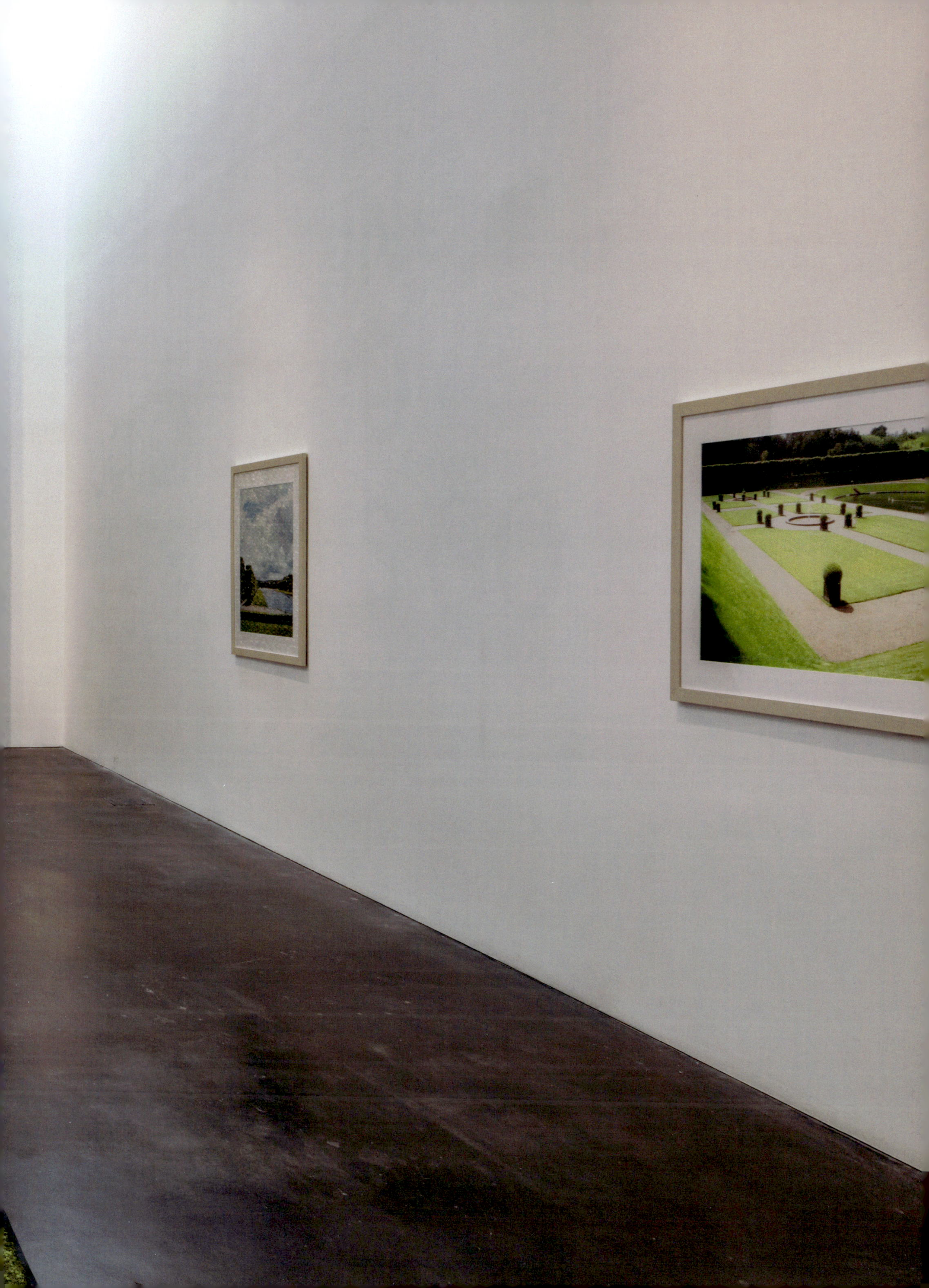

Checklist of the Exhibition

Lady J (Model #4), 1994/1999.
Porcelain, 3 × 7 ½ × 3 inches.
Courtesy the artist.

PAGES 55, 67, 84–85

Lady J (Bear Claw), 1996/2000.
Porcelain, 2 × 5 ½ × 4 inches.
Courtesy Sharon Collias.

PAGES 55, 67, 84–85

Lady J (Cornea #2), 1996/2014.
Porcelain, 3 × 6 ½ × 2 ¼ inches.
Courtesy the artist.

PAGES 49, 55, 67, 84–85

Slipper, 1996.
Porcelain, 3 × 7 × 4 inches.
Courtesy the artist.

PAGES 55, 67, 84–85

Banana Tree, 1997.
Glazed stoneware, 32 ¼ × 11 inches.
Courtesy the artist and Robischon Gallery, Denver.

PAGES 68, 78

Jacqueline's Lady J in Use, 1997.
Framed Polaroid, 14 × 11 ½ inches.
Photograph by India Dunnington.
Courtesy the artist.

PAGES 55, 67, 84–85

Jen's Lady J in Use, 1997.
Framed Polaroid, 14 × 11 ½ inches.
Photograph by Eric Baum
Courtesy the artist.

PAGES 55, 67, 84–85

Jen's Lady J in Use, 1997.
Framed Polaroid, 14 × 11 ½ inches.
Photograph by Eric Baum.
Courtesy the artist.

PAGES 55, 67, 84–85

Jen's Lady J in Use, 1997.
Framed Polaroid, 14 × 11 ½ inches.
Photograph by Eric Baum.
Courtesy the artist.

PAGES 55, 67, 84–85

Lady J (Push-Me-Pull-You), 1997.
Porcelain, 3 × 7 ½ × 2 ¾ inches.
Courtesy Stacy Greene.

PAGES 55, 67, 84–85

Michele's Lady J in Use, 1997.
Framed Polaroid, 14 × 11 ½ inches.
Photograph by Merrick Pratt.
Courtesy the artist.

PAGES 55, 67, 84–85

Nick's Nursing Bottle in Use, 1997.
Framed Polaroid, 11 × 9 inches.
Courtesy the artist.

PAGE 67

Nursing Bottles (for Men), 1997.
Porcelain, *Chocolate* (3 × 4 × 4 ½ inches), *White* (1 × 2 ¼ × 3 inches).
Courtesy the artist.

PAGES 66–67

Phoenix Bottle, 1997.
Glazed stoneware, 32 ½ × 16 inches.
Courtesy the artist and Robischon Gallery, Denver.

PAGE 78

Pissoir (Female Model), 1997.
Porcelain, 2 × 6 × 3 ½ inches.
Courtesy Stacy Greene.

PAGES 55, 67, 84–85

Pissoir (Male Model), 1997.
Porcelain, 2 ½ × 6 ½ × 3 inches.
Courtesy Stacy Greene.

PAGES 55, 67, 84–85

Stacy's Lady J in Use, 1997
Framed Polaroid, 14 × 11 ½ inches.
Photograph by Maria Levitsky.
Courtesy the artist.

PAGES 55, 67, 84–85

Stacy's Lady J in Use (Female Model), 1997.
Framed Polaroid, 14 × 11 ½ inches.
Photograph by Kim Dickey.
Courtesy the artist.

PAGES 55, 67, 84–85

Cascade, 1999.
Porcelain, 3 × 7 × 3 inches.
Courtesy the artist.

PAGES 55, 67, 84–85

Sprinkle, 1999.
Porcelain, 3 × 7 ½ × 1 ½ inches.
Courtesy the artist.

PAGES 55, 67, 84–85

Havisham Bride, 2000.
Glazed stoneware, 33 ¼ × 15 ½ inches.
Collection of Deborah Dell and Scott Chamberlin.

PAGES 68, 78

Pocket Lady: You Only Have One Chance, 2000.
Velvet, tulle, leather, various objects, 66 inches neck to hem.
Courtesy the artist.

PAGES 67, 73

Shotgun Bride, 2000.
Glazed porcelain, 32 ¼ × 15 inches.
Courtesy Jeanne Quinn.

PAGE 78

The Fall, 2000.
Video, TRT 13 minutes.
Written and co-directed by Kim Dickey.
Starring Peter Halasz as the Devil and Kim Dickey as servant.
Chefs: David Pasternack and Eileen Green; Cameraman and Co-Director: Dan Walworth; Music and Sound Design: Brain Dewan and Subvoyant; Edited by Mauren Donohue and Ken Rosenberg; Production assistants: Joe Amrhein and Stacy Greene; Still photography: David Scher.
Courtesy the artist.

PAGES 52–53

The Fall Set, 2000.
Porcelain, 9 × 20 × 15 inches.
Courtesy the artist.

PAGES 53, 83

Woman in White, 2000.
Glazed stoneware, 37 ½ × 14 inches.
Courtesy the Estate of Robin Rule.

PAGES 68, 78

Beauty Bush, 2002.
Glazed terracotta and Douglas fir, 19 × 19 inches.
Courtesy the artist and Robischon Gallery, Denver.

PAGES 18, 24, 76

Rosebud Bush, 2002.
Glazed terracotta, 30 × 26 inches.
Courtesy the artist and Robischon Gallery, Denver.

PAGES 20, 24, 88

Schneeballen, 2002.
Glazed terracotta, 16 × 18 inches.
Courtesy the artist.

PAGES 24, 66, 73

Salad Plate Series: Green, Mixed, Spun and *Tossed*, 2003.
Color lithographs, each 9 × 11 inches.
Courtesy Shark's Ink, Lyons, CO.

PAGES 66, 82

Lift and Divide, 2005.
Printed industrial rug, 6 × 10 feet.
Courtesy the artist and Robischon Gallery.

PAGES 24, 88

Leaf-Fringed Legend, 2006.
Glazed stoneware, 49 × 15 inches.
Courtesy Mark Falcone and Ellen Bruss.

PAGE 79

Box Construction (Villandry), 2007.
Light jet print from 2 ¼-inch film, 36 × 36 inches.
Courtesy the artist.

PAGE 27

Corridor (Versailles), 2007.
Light jet print from 2 ¼-inch film, 36 × 36 inches.
Courtesy the artist.

PAGE 88

Expanded Field (Villandry), 2007.
Light jet print from 2 ¼-inch film, 42 × 40 inches.
Courtesy the artist.

PAGE 26

Extended Recess (Villandry), 2007.
Light jet print from 2 ¼-inch film, 30 × 42 inches.

PAGE 88

First Course, 2007.
Glazed porcelain, 21 ¾ × 2 ½ inches.
Courtesy Lisa Albright.

PAGE 77

Green Altar, 2007.
Glazed porcelain, 31 ½ × 11 inches.
Courtesy Mark Falcone and Ellen Bruss.

PAGES 27, 78

Square Grotto (Fontainebleau), 2007.
Light jet print from 2 ¼-inch film, 36 × 36 inches.
Courtesy the artist.
PAGE 88

Pucker, 2008.
Glazed porcelain, 30 × 13 inches.
Anonymous.
PAGES 68, 79

Inverted L Beam, 2010.
Aluminum, glazed terracotta, silicone, and rubber grommets, 46 × 46 × 17 inches.
Courtesy the artist and Robischon Gallery, Denver.
PAGES 14, 31, 69

Step, 2010.
Aluminum, glazed terracotta, silicone, and rubber grommets, 51 × 38 × 38 inches.
Courtesy the artist and Robischon Gallery, Denver.
PAGE 14

Corner, 2011.
Aluminum, glazed terracotta, silicone, and rubber grommets, 24 × 36 × 36 inches.
Courtesy the artist and Robischon Gallery, Denver.
PAGES 14, 36, 76

I Beam, 2011.
Aluminum, glazed terracotta, silicone, and rubber grommets, 8 ¼ × 122 × 8 ¼ inches.
Courtesy the artist and Robischon Gallery, Denver.
PAGES 14, 31, 69

Inverted L Beam #2, 2011.
Aluminum, glazed terracotta, silicone, and rubber grommets, 78 × 137 ½ × 17 inches.
Courtesy the artist and Robischon Gallery, Denver.
PAGES 11, 80–81

Plan for *Cold Pastoral*, 2011.
Paper collage, 10 × 40 inches.
Courtesy the artist.

Parterre, 2012.
Aluminum, glazed terracotta, silicone, and rubber grommets, 15 × 15 × 1 ¾ feet.
Courtesy the artist.
PAGES 41–43, 88

Rest Assured, X Boyfriends, 2014.
Denim, cotton batting, thread, and expired condoms, 130 × 86 inches.
Courtesy the artist.
PAGES 66, 72

To the Fullness of the Day (and Pale Illuminations of the Night), 2014.
Glazed stoneware, 26 × 13 ½ inches.
Courtesy the artist and Robischon Gallery, Denver.
PAGE 79

Clan Champion (Probity after R. Frost), 2015.
Glazed stoneware and powder-coated steel, 12 × 20 ½ × 16 inches.
Courtesy the artist and Robischon Gallery, Denver.
PAGES 36, 75, 86, 87

Fading Bouquet, 2015.
Glazed stoneware, 32 × 15 inches.
Courtesy the artist and Robischon Gallery, Denver.
PAGES 17, 68, 78

Illusory Bouquet, 2015.
Glazed stoneware, 34 × 16 inches.
Courtesy the artist and Robischon Gallery, Denver.
PAGE 78

Nightwatch (Blind Perception after V. Hugo), 2015.
Glazed stoneware and powder-coated steel, 15 × 13 × 18 inches.
Courtesy the artist and Robischon Gallery, Denver.
PAGE 87

No Resting (Determination), 2015.
Glazed stoneware and powder-coated steel, 23 × 14 × 12 inches.
Courtesy the artist and Robischon Gallery, Denver.

PAGES 36, 87

Omphalos, 2015.
Glazed terracotta, 30 × 1 inches.
Courtesy the artist and Robischon Gallery, Denver.

PAGES 36, 56

The Collector (Memory), 2015.
Glazed stoneware and powder-coated steel, 12 × 13 × 13 inches.
Courtesy the artist and Robischon Gallery, Denver.

PAGE 87

The Girlfriend (Fidelity), 2015.
Glazed stoneware and powder-coated steel, 11 × 14 ¼ × 18 inches.
Courtesy the artist and Robischon Gallery, Denver.

PAGES 75, 87

Travelling Companion (Endurance), 2015.
Glazed stoneware and powder-coated steel, 12 × 17 ¾ × 15 ¼ inches.
Courtesy the artist and Robischon Gallery, Denver.

PAGE 87

At Your Service (the Intolerability of Chains for A. Davis), 2016.
Glazed stoneware and powder-coated steel, 27 × 15 × 14 inches.
Courtesy the artist and Robischon Gallery, Denver.

PAGES 74, 86, 87

Deadly Force (the Predatory), 2016.
Glazed stoneware and powder-coated steel, 22 × 16 × 22 inches.
Courtesy the artist and Robischon Gallery, Denver.

PAGES 74, 86, 87

Homeland Security, 2016.
Glazed stoneware and powder-coated steel, 16 ½ × 12 × 10 ½ inches.
Courtesy the artist and Robischon Gallery, Denver.

PAGES 75, 87

Lineage, 2016.
Site-specific charcoal wall drawing, dimensions variable.
Courtesy the artist.

PAGES 74–75, 86–87

The 13th Labor (Domesticated Wild Boar), 2016.
Glazed stoneware and powder-coated steel, 13 × 13 ½ × 13 ½ inches.
Courtesy the artist and Robischon Gallery, Denver.

PAGE 87

The Hunt, 2016.
Glazed terracotta, *Woman pointing through the Bushes* (25 ¾ × 21 inches), *Dog with Net* (26 ½ × 24 ¼ inches), *Woman with escaping Rabbit* (36 ½ × 22 inches), *Caught* (35 ¾ × 21 inches).
Courtesy the artist and Robischon Gallery, Denver.

PAGES 70–71

The Impossibility of Letting Go, 2016.
Glazed stoneware and powder-coated steel, 18 × 17 × 17 inches.
Courtesy the artist and Robischon Gallery, Denver.

PAGE 87

Time Out (When in Doubt Wash for P. Gallico), 2016.
Glazed stoneware and powder-coated steel, 13 × 16 × 14 inches.
Courtesy the artist and Robischon Gallery, Denver.

PAGES 75, 87

Acknowledgments

MCA Denver gratefully acknowledges the Elizabeth Firestone Graham Foundation for its support of this publication. The museum thanks the Foundation for its singular role in championing the work of artists at pivotal stages in their career.

This publication would not be possible without the efforts of the team at Lucia|Marquand: Adrian Lucia, Melissa Duffes, Kestrel Rundle, and Leah Finger all worked diligently to ensure the book was completed on time. Ryan Polich's patience and collaborative spirit brought a beautiful design to life and this book is a testament to his sensitive understanding of Kim Dickey's work.

The exhibition at MCA Denver included several loans for which we are grateful: Lisa Albright, Ellen Bruss & Mark Falcone, Scott Chamberlin & Deborah Dell, Sharon Collias, the Estate of Robin Rule, Baryn Futa, Stacy Greene, and Jeanne Quinn all lent important work to this presentation. We also thank Robischon Gallery and Rule Gallery for their vital assistance with all manner of logistical details.

MCA Denver's Board of Trustees has long been committed to celebrating the work of artists in this region and their support of this exhibition is a terrific acknowledgement of that. I am grateful to Adam Lerner, Director and Chief Animator, for his encouragement of this project. Zoe Larkins and Nick Silici contributed immensely to the clarity of this book and the elegant installation of the exhibition.

Lastly, I wish to thank Kim Dickey for her tremendous efforts in realizing this project. The generosity with which she shared her ideas, her work, and her vision for the installation and publication has been profound. MCA Denver is honored to present this ambitious and thought-provoking work to museum visitors and readers now.

Contributors

Glenn Adamson is an independent scholar in New York.

Lisa Tamiris Becker was the Director of the Abroms-Engel Institute for the Visual Arts.

Elissa Auther is the Windgate Research Curator at the Museum of Arts and Design and the Bard Graduate Center.

Ezra Shales is Professor at the Massachusetts College of Art and Design.

Nora Burnett Abrams is Curator at the Museum of Contemporary Art Denver.

This book is published in conjunction with the exhibition *Kim Dickey: Words Are Leaves,* presented at MCA Denver from October 8, 2016 to January 22, 2017.

Library of Congress Control Number: 2016951875
ISBN 978-0-692-76221-9

Published by MCA Denver
www.mcadenver.org

Available through:
ARTBOOK | D.A.P.
155 6th Avenue, 2nd Floor
New York, NY 10013
www.artbook.com

Produced by Lucia|Marquand, Seattle
www.luciamarquand.com

Edited by Nora Burnett Abrams
Designed by Ryan Polich
Typeset in Chronicle Display and Calluna by Kestrel Rundle
Proofread by Elissa Greisz
Color management by iocolor, Seattle
Printed and bound in China by Artron Art Group

Photography credits:
Front cover: *Mille-fleur* (detail), 2011. Aluminum, glazed terracotta, silicone, and rubber grommets, 85 × 242 × 15 inches. Crystal Bridges Museum of American Art, Bentonville, Arkansas, 2015.6. Photograph by Marc F. Henning.
Pages 2–3: Photograph by Nick Havholm.
Page 4: Photograph by Kim Dickey.
Back cover: *Galla Placida*, 2007. Glazed terracotta on limestone, 30 × 24 inches. Photography courtesy Studio Penumbra.